On-Demand Publishing

On-Demand Publishing

Second Edition

toExcel
San Jose   New York   Lincoln   Shanghai

On-Demand Publishing

All Rights Reserved. Copyright © 1999 toExcel

No part of this book may be reproduced or transmitted in any form or by any means, graphic, electronic, or mechanical, including photocopying, recording, taping, or by any information storage or retrieval system, without the permission in writing from the publisher.

For information address:
toExcel
165 West 95th Street, Suite B-N
New York, NY 10025
www.toExcel.com

ISBN: 1-58348-152-4

Printed in the United States of America

0 9 8 7 6 5 4 3 2

"Look, then, into thine heart, and write!"

Henry Wadsworth Longfellow 1807–1882
Voices of the Night. Prelude

Contents

About toExcel

Foreword

Chapter 1
The On-Demand Publishing Revolution   3
    The beauty of the book
    What is on-demand publishing?
    Who can benefit?
    Pressing the Internet advantage

Chapter 2
The New Paradigm   13
    Technologies for new and old books
    Printing
    Book selling
    The economic case
    On-demand versus vanity publishing
    The product of the equation

Chapter 3
Publishing with toExcel   25
    OP authors return to their public
    Case study: Danny Goodman

    International publishers open new markets
    Case studies: Éditions du Rocher and Tachibana Publishing Group

University presses in the vanguard
Case studies: Harvard and Columbia universities

Traditional publishers get more books on the list
Case study: The Coriolis Group

toExcel's publishing partners

Chapter 4
A New Way to Get Published 43
No rejection letters from The People's Press
Marketing your book
Case studies
How it works
toExcel's authors

Chapter 5
toExcel's Own Book Series 57
The Open Documents and Open Source Libraries
The New Millennium Library
The Open Stories Series
The edUniverse–University of Nebraska–Lincoln Learning Series

Epilogue 65
The Future of On-Demand Publishing

Appendix 69
toExcel Publishing Services Procedures (rev. 3/22/99)

About toExcel

What we do

toExcel's mission is simple. We provide access to books. You, the reader, tell us what you're interested in and we'll work to acquire it for easy viewing. If you want to take the process a step further and print the material in a quality book format, then there's a good chance we'll do that too.

Our focus is on the millions of titles and manuscripts being ignored by today's mass-market publishers. This includes out-of-print titles, foreign language selections, and high-quality material focused for specific audiences. It also includes fiction and nonfiction from every imaginable source—whether from award-winning professional, an aspiring writer, or a teenage novice. We have developed the world's most efficient publishing processes for authors and publishers alike, and we're willing to take chances. We're launching a democratic revolution in publishing—an opportunity for publishing professionals and authors to reach new audiences and a chance for readers to define what interests them. *We do all this through our publishing supersite, toExcel.com.

We also realize that many valuable experiences and insights are too concentrated to be put in a standard book format. That's why we have developed our OpenStories program that provides people with a flexible way to impart their insight or knowledge as part of an anthology with other contributors.

* Note: toExcel will not publish or provide access to hate-related or sexually abusive material.

Company history

toExcel was launched in late 1998. The company's strategic foundation grew out of an education, training, and publishing company that was founded in late 1996.

The company includes a unique mix of people from the education, publishing, computer, and information technology industries. It currently has operations in San Jose, California; Lincoln, Nebraska; New York City; and Shanghai, China. The company has on-demand printing relationships in the Americas and Europe and plans to expand the capability into Asia during the next twelve months.

The company currently employs over 200 people. The operational fundamentals were finalized in mid-1998 and the Web site launched later that year. The ReaderCentral, WriterCentral, PublishCentral, and OpenStories areas were launched in early 1999.

Business opportunities

We are always interested in new publishing ideas and business proposals. If you have a book, idea, or business proposal please contact us.

Employment opportunities

Our company is a fast-paced start-up with a strong team environment. We are looking for energetic individuals interested in helping us reinvent the publishing industry. We currently have opportunities in the following areas:

Editorial advisors

toExcel is looking for editorial representatives for upcoming categories in our OpenStories online forum. Interested individuals should have a minimum of three years of editing and content selection experience. Web familiarity is highly desirable. The position is freelance and geographically insensitive.

Marketing associates

toExcel is looking for self-motivated individuals interested in working with the company to expand domestic and international markets. Candidates will develop and manage various integrated marketing programs including but not limited to collateral, direct mail, events, and sales tools. They will be called on to contribute excellent writing and editing skills.

Contact toExcel

toExcel
165 West 95th Street, Suite B-N
New York, NY 10025
www.toExcel.com

1-877-82EXCEL

Foreword

How publishing will change
by Gregg Williams

True, the world will not change overnight, and certain aspects of publishing will stay the same. Authors will still submit books to companies like Random House and Simon & Schuster. Some of these books (a very few) will be printed in advance and shipped, en masse, to bookstores across the country. There will still be a *New York Times* bestseller list, and getting a book listed there will still be an impressive accomplishment.

Having said that, I must return to my original statement. Publishing *will* change dramatically, because of a new publishing model called *Internet-based publishing* (IBP). toExcel, with its Open Publishing platform, is the first company to make IBP both possible and affordable, and I am very excited about the possibilities that now exist because of toExcel's publishing services. People now have widespread access to being published, and this will be a positive change overall—although we will have to change our ideas about what "being published" really means.

Getting published

Until the advent of IBP, you had two options: commercial publishing and self-publishing. Trying to get your book (of whatever sort) published commercially was—and will always be—a difficult process full of disappointment and frustration. Because of the built-in limitations of the industry, only a fraction of the books submitted get published, and books of great merit often remain unpublished.

At the other end of the spectrum, you could self-publish your book, a process costing several thousands of dollars that usually left you with a garage full of copies and no way to sell them.

Two things change all that. First, the Internet has become a decentralized conduit for communicating and doing business with other people, worldwide. Second, digital storage of books (and complementary content-delivery technologies) makes it possible for books to be stored, ready for purchase, at minimal cost. (With a one-time fee of $299, toExcel does an excellent job of making publication affordable.)

Put the two together, and you get IBP, which drives the cost of "being published," pre-sale, to a modest amount. This means that, for the first time in history, *virtually any author can offer her book to a large fraction of the world's population without being blocked from doing so.*

Different kinds of publishing

IBP will bring the "Wild West" innovation of the Internet into to the publishing world. Before, there was only self-publishing and commercial publishing. Soon, you will see as many models of publishing as there are people who think them up.

Right now, toExcel (through its People's Press program) makes it possible for you to self-publish your book—but with the advantage that the general public can buy your book over the Internet or by special-ordering them from any brick-and-mortar bookstore.

But by working with toExcel, it's also possible for someone with a modest amount of money to become her own publisher and publish books according to whatever criteria she wishes.

In the future, you will be able to choose from a variety of publishing models. Here are some possibilities:

- "unconditional" publishing (whatever you want published gets published) for a flat fee

- unconditional publishing for a lower per-month fee (perhaps more economical for time-sensitive information or books that need to be widely available for a limited period of time)

- "assisted" unconditional publishing (a form of "uncritical" publishing that includes various kinds of editorial assistance)

- "guild" publishing (you join a writer's guild, and your book gets published only if it meets the guild's approval—but such books have a better reputation than unconditionally published books)
- "professional" publishing (which just like traditional publishing in that the publisher decides whether or not to publish your book)

And, of course, each of these varieties of publishing can come in various "flavors," with various costs and payment rates based on the amount of copy editing, structural advice, and book promotion involved.

What will "getting published" mean?

Obviously, the connotations of "getting published" will change. Today, the term "published author" is definitely a mark of distinction that sets you apart from the unwashed (or, perhaps, unpublished) masses. The very fact that you have been published means that someone (namely, your publisher) thinks that what you have to say is more important or worthwhile than what a number of other people had to say—and they're willing to risk serious money to make sure you get heard.

You can see that, once IBP becomes more prevalent, "getting published" will not necessarily have the same glamour it has today—after all, virtually anyone who perseveres long enough to write a book can see it published. Getting published will retain its status in two ways: first, when the status emanates from the status of the publisher, and second, when readers recognize the inherent value of what the author has written.

This second source of prestige is at the heart of how IBP will change publishing:

Everyone has a chance to be heard, and success is more a matter of what you have to say than whether or not you can successfully pass through the gantlet of the traditional publisher.

Will this completely level the playing field? No—you will have to work hard to let the world know about what you have to offer, and money spent on advertising will still increase your chance of success. But the situation will be better than what it is now.

Redefining "success"

Maybe it's time to redefine what success is. If you have defined success as "selling a million copies and getting rich," the odds are still largely against you. Yes, it could happen—and toExcel makes eventual success more of a possibility than it is today. Your book could build a readership across the years and be "discovered" by the reviewer of the New York Times ten years from now. That certainly can't happen today—you get one printing, one shot at success.

But the situation looks better if you redefine what constitutes success. Many people simply want to be heard. They want to tell a story that's important to them. With toExcel, they now have a chance. Maybe their sphere of influence spreads only as far as their family or their community. That could be far enough. Sometimes, one person with the right idea can still change the world.

I know an executive who has a book—a children's book, written to a young daughter that he gets to spend too little time with. This man can now get his book published. And once in print, it can be saved and given to her when she's older. One would hope that she would keep it, read it, and think of her father in a different way because of that book. Perhaps she might even read it to her children someday. Success, for this man, is not measured in fame and money; it's measured in being remembered. He has a great chance of being successful.

If you are thinking about writing a book, I wish you well. It is hard work, but you will definitely learn something from the experience. (I'm fond of saying that, with the possible exceptions of Isaac Asimov and Stephen King, nobody enjoys writing, but everybody enjoys having written.) If you have written a book, the very fact of completing it—no matter what else happens—is something to be proud of.

In either case, I ask you to ponder what you hope to accomplish by publishing your book. If you have a clear and realistic answer to this question, you will have a much greater chance of being pleased with the results of your publishing venture.

Internet-based publishing makes it possible for anyone to be successfully published—and that's why it will change the world.

Gregg Williams is the site manager of Pubspace (www.pubspace.com), a noncommercial site that covers the field of Internet-based publishing. You can reach Gregg Williams at manager@pubspace.com. Copyright 1999 by Gregg Williams; all rights reserved.

*"Of all those arts in which the wise excel,
Nature's chief masterpiece is writing
well."*

Sheffield, Duke of Buckinghamshire. 1649–1720
Essay on Poetry

Chapter 1

The On-Demand Publishing Revolution

With 90,000 books going out-of-print each year, with over twenty million U.S. adults interested in creative writing, with half a million non-English titles being generated each year, the time for a new way of publishing, for on-demand publishing, is now. Hundreds of authors and publishers are already working with toExcel to get their books in print and reaching the marketplace quickly and effectively. Why? It works. It's fast, inexpensive and high quality. It's the way of the future.

- The entire U.S. publishing industry produced only 54,000 titles in 1997, down from 62,000 in 1995.
- toExcel published over 250 titles in its first few months of operation and is on track to publish more than 10,000 titles in 1999.

Millions of people worldwide have "the dream" of being published, but few ever succeed. Almost ninety percent of completed manuscripts in America never make it to print. They are locked out by the restrictive economics of traditional publishing—an antiquated system in which publishers spend more money deciding what books to publish than on advances for their authors. A system that spends huge sums printing, transporting and warehousing the large number of books that never get sold. A system that excludes any book that can't guarantee sales in the thousands.

Ever wonder what happens to all those books in stores that don't sell? The stores simply return them to the publisher who reduces them to pulp. Hanging to these old ways of traditional publishing just doesn't make sense in this day and age when new technologies have changed almost every other business and every other aspect of our lives. That's why toExcel has integrated a group of cutting-edge technologies to create an Open Publishing Platform™ that allows every author to publish a book. A real book.

The beauty of the book

Some have argued that the Internet, which has no printing, transportation, and warehousing costs, will make traditional publishing obsolete. But people aren't ready to give up the ease and pleasure of reading traditional books.

There is something magical about a book that makes it different from every other form for exchanging information. As we head toward the twenty-first century, no one can claim that books are the best way to store information or to transfer knowledge, but books still play a huge role in our lives. People have a passion for reading good books that they don't have about reading information off of a computer screen. They spend hours browsing in bookstores on Sunday afternoons with no particular purchase in mind. In fact, many bookstores now house reading rooms and coffee shops to accommodate these all-day browsers.

The growth of massive bookstore chains like Barnes & Noble and Borders, and electronic bookstores like *barnesandnoble.com* and *Amazon.com* have made it clear that the Internet will not make the book obsolete. Instead, the technology that makes the Internet possible will, when combined with new printing technologies and vision, change the entire publishing industry. And, it won't be the first time that technology has revolutionized publishing—and changed our lives in a major way.

When Johannes Gutenberg invented the printing press, he changed almost every aspect of the way people live. He changed the way we looked at the world, the way we learned, the role religion played in our society, and the way information was collected and exchanged. He changed both the economics and technology of publishing, but he didn't change one key reality—over 500 years after his invention, many good authors *still* can't get their books published.

Before the invention of the printing press in 1452, books were actually manuscripts reproduced by hand, usually by monks working long hours alone in their monasteries. Because of the extraordinary time needed to produce each book, only the chosen few could be completed. That economic reality (and the monks' control of which manuscripts were selected) meant that, for the most part, only Bibles and other religious works were transcribed.

Secular books such as textbooks, new philosophies, and novels, were unavailable to the common man. Philosophers and thinkers lacked an efficient medium to promulgate their new ideas. Storytellers had no way to tell their tales to the masses.

Although Gutenberg's invention gave us a valuable tool for mass distribution of ideas, many thinkers, educators and storytellers are still looking for ways to get their ideas and tales in print and into the hands of a mass audience. This pent-up demand for a truly democratic medium—one in which anyone can make his or her voice heard—is one of the driving forces behind the explosion in popularity of the Internet and the World Wide Web.

The Web has pushed technology a step further by making it possible for almost anyone to get his work published electronically. But this new reality still doesn't make "the dream" possible. Most people don't dream of the day when they will create their first Web site. They don't usually celebrate when one of their friends becomes a Webmaster. No. They want to be *authors*. They want their name on the cover of a *book*, because publishing a book possesses a quality and confers a status that the Web has never had and perhaps never will.

Documents published on the Web lack the ease and flexibility of use of that tremendous piece of technology, the traditional book. It's so easy and gratifying to read a trashy novel on the beach or a good thriller on the subway. Who wants to read an entire novel from a computer screen? In addition, the Web also still lacks the universal reach of traditional print. For as quickly as the Internet has grown, it is still used by a small minority of our planet's population.

Yes, there are breakthroughs in display technology and electronic reading devices that will soon be available at affordable prices. But when more than a few pages of content are involved, even Bill Gates admits that he prints out electronic information in order to read it. Even with the clearest and most portable of monitors, there is no substitute for the bound book.

Today, the new technologies behind the Internet, combined with advances in printing technology, provide a new and practical solution for unpublished authors: on-demand publishing. Finally, the technology exists to make "the dream" achievable for everyone.

What is on-demand publishing?

On-demand publishing has changed the economics of publishing, making it possible to publish books without having to guarantee that they will sell thousands of copies—a guarantee needed by traditional publishers who have to cover massive printing, shipping, and warehousing expenses each time they print a book. With on-demand publishing, books that only sell a few dozen copies can earn a profit for both authors and publishers.

toExcel's Open Publishing Platform™ epitomizes the on-demand publishing revolution. It's a combination of people, technology, distribution, and marketing expertise that enables anyone, from individuals to businesses to educational institutions, to publish easily and affordably without worrying about the huge capital investment and inventory risk associated with long-run traditional publishing.

It is, quite simply, state-of-the-art on-demand printing technology combined with the power of people and the Web that opens the publishing world to anyone with ideas to express. It changes the fundamental economics of publishing by reducing the cost of entry, while providing substantial financial rewards for success.

Here's how it works.

- Authors and publishers agree to publish with toExcel.
- Our designers and technicians take existing books or digital manuscripts and create a set of professional-looking, print-ready digital files that are stored and ready for on-demand printing.
- Books are available for sale through a distribution agreement with Ingram Book Company and can be bought online, on the phone, via

fax and in virtually any bookstore in the world that orders through Ingram.

- Books are printed when ordered and shipped within 48 hours.
- Books can be read in their entirety at the toExcel Web site, which promotes sales.
- Web marketing tools are provided to help authors, publishers and organizations sell their books using toExcel's e-commerce capability.
- All administration, accounting, shipping, and other "factory" operations are handled by toExcel.
- Authors, organizations, and publishers are paid top royalties for each copy sold.

Who can benefit?

On-demand publishing makes it possible to publish books that would have been financially impossible to publish in the past. New authors can make their voices heard, academics can publish books on niche topics with a small readership, and an array of foreign-language books can be published profitably for the U.S. market. Virtually anyone or any group can benefit.

New authors, previously published authors and all types of publishers can benefit from toExcel's Open Publishing Platform. Publishers like Harvard University Press, Columbia University Press, Tachibana Shuppan, Éditions du Rocher, East China Normal University, Fudan University, and Coriolis, as well as authors Danny Goodman, Col. John Warden, professor Ron Gilster, and hundreds more have already joined the toExcel publishing revolution.

Not only can new books reach the market quickly via on-demand publishing, but existing out-of-print books by authors who have already succeeded in getting published in the traditional way can get a new life. Many published but unheralded authors watch helplessly as their books go into literary limbo soon after they are published. Bookstores send the unsold copies back to publisher for credit, and customers who want to buy that book are told that it is out-of-print or out-of-stock. The book, for all intents and purposes, is dead.

With toExcel, existing out-of-print and in-print books can be stored electronically after their traditional life is over, making them available to buyers across North America. They are no longer dead: they are given eternal life through digitization, electronic storage and on-demand printing.

International publishers with existing in-print or out-of-print books can open new markets in North American by republishing with toExcel, while university presses and traditional publishers can use toExcel's Open Publishing Platform™ successfully republish books with smaller or niche markets.

Pressing the Internet advantage

Not only is new technology used in the creation of toExcel books, it is also used in the marketing and sales of those books. As *barnesandnoble.com* and *amazon.com* have proven, the Internet is a powerful tool for selling books. It is a superb tool for delivering information about books arranged in searchable databases. Instead of hunting through several bookstores to find what they want, readers can now log onto the Web and buy almost any book they want. They can also get information on books from publishers, authors and other readers.

The Web also provides authors with an exciting medium for marketing their books. Authors can create a personalized home page that explains who they are and what their book is about. They can then work to get that home page linked to similar pages around the Web and build their own audience and fan club. Although Internet marketing may not reach the sheer numbers that traditional marketing can, it can reach the author's niche audience—people who are actually interested in the book. Plus, Web marketing can be done much less expensively than using traditional marketing, and it gives the author, the person who knows the book the best. more control.

toExcel has created a turnkey system, an Open Publishing Platform™, that allows any author to get published, and assists publishers and already-published authors in keeping their books from falling into the purgatory of out-of-print/out-of-stock status. toExcel has created its own imprints to help get new authors into print and to make otherwise unavailable books accessible to North American book buyers.

While on-demand publishing may not revolutionize our lives the way the printing press did, it does promise to follow in Gutenberg's footsteps, using new technology to create new economics and new opportunities. And it promises to finally make "the dream" of publishing available to everyone.

"Art is long, life short; judgment difficult, opportunity transient."

Goethe. 1749–1832
Book vii. Chap. ix.

Chapter 2

The New Paradigm

On-demand publishing, the industry's new paradigm, is based on a simple equation:

new technology + new economics = new opportunities.

It revolutionized the publishing industry in the fifteenth century, and it is doing it again today—at toExcel.

When Gutenberg created the printing press, he didn't invent a single new technology—he brought together several existing technologies in a new way. toExcel's Open Publishing Platform™ integrates both new and existing scanning, storage, printing, e-commerce, and Internet technologies to change the way books are published.

Today's technology has made books printed on-demand indistinguishable from traditionally printed books. All toExcel books look exactly like books printed using traditional offset printing systems. That's one reason why toExcel is the leader in on-demand publishing.

It may sound a little far-fetched to think that some fancy new printers and the Internet will completely revolutionize a business as old as the publishing industry. But smaller, less impressive pieces of equipment have brought major changes to publishing in the past.

The last time a new technology revolutionized the marketing and sale of books as much as on-demand publishing technologies was in the early 1970s when Ingram Book Company first employed the microfiche reader to provide better service to its bookstore customers.

For years, due to the sheer size of the United States, wholesalers had a good business filling reorders for the fastest-moving books. Before the Ingram microfiche changed the industry, wholesalers didn't have an incentive to stock many titles other than the best sellers. This resulted in a business climate between bookstores and wholesalers filled with mutual frustration and disappointment, because wholesalers would routinely find that they had only thirty percent of the books ordered actually in stock. Bookstores, in those pre-digital days would have to wait a week or more to find out which seventy books they weren't going to get.

All this changed when Harry Hoffman, the president of Ingram Book Company, then an insignificant wholesaler in Nashville, Tennessee, discovered the microfiche reader, a clunky slide projector kind of machine. The value of the microfiche reader was that it permitted a huge amount of information to be stored on a very small piece of film.

That one small machine completely changed the way bookstores, wholesalers and publishers did business. In 1970, there were dozens, if not hundreds, of wholesalers in America bigger than Ingram. Today there are none.

If a microfiche machine can rewrite the rules of book distribution, just imagine what the technology behind on-demand printing can do.

Technologies for new and old books

New technology lets toExcel bring out-of-print books back to life—and put them in-print forever. First, the actual pages of the book block are scanned to digital files using the latest Xerox hardware and software. The digital files are corrected using patented toExcel technologies. We can even add a new introduction or epilogue to the book that puts it into context for new readers—as we did for Col. John Warden's recent update of his book on U.S. military war strategy, *The Air Campaign*. This new edition would have been prohibitively expensive and time-consuming using traditional offset printing technology.

If needed, a new four-color cover is created for the book by toExcel cover designers. If not, the original cover is scanned, retouched and color-corrected for the ICC profile of the digital printer. toExcel updates any text on the cover. Finally, a new EAN barcode is created and placed on the back cover along with the toExcel and printer's logos.

toExcel designs new books from new manuscripts submitted to toExcel as digital files created in a popular word-processing application. Once accepted, toExcel's graphic engineers and cover designers use state-of-the-art software to design the manuscript and create a unique, four-color cover as described above.

Complete specifications for submitting existing books and new manuscripts for publication by toExcel can be found at www.toExcel.com.

Once a book has been recreated as a full complement of print-ready, digital files, those files are sent to our printing facility where proof copies are printed. The book then becomes orderable though the Ingram Books database. The files reside in a digital storage facility until ordered from our Web site, another online book seller or from a traditional bookstore. Once ordered, the book is printed, bound and shipped—usually within forty-eight hours.

Printing

The cornerstone printing technology behind toExcel's on-demand publishing is a new series of printers that can produce bookstore-quality books inexpensively and quickly. Both IBM and Xerox now produce printers capable of creating perfect-bound, books with four-color, laminated soft covers that are indistinguishable from books produced using traditional offset printing methods.

There are two parts to every book, the cover and everything else in between—what we call the "book block." Both IBM and Xerox have created software and hardware packages that can store libraries of digital files and print from them as soon as a customer orders a book. Books can be created in several sizes, from a traditional novel size of 5" x 8" or 5½" x 8½" to larger "manual" sizes 6" x 9" and 7½" x 9¼" as well as the standard 8½" x 11".

The technology available to toExcel for creating professional-looking book blocks and covers is perhaps one of the most important reasons on-demand publishing is now a reality. Who would want to publish his novel if it looked like it had been made on a photocopier?

Thanks to advances in printing technology, on-demand books can look as good, if not better, than traditionally produced books.

Most toExcel books are currently printed at Lightning Print, a subsidiary of Ingram Book Company in LaVergne, Tennessee, outside of Nashville. The book blocks are printed from digital files on the IBM's InfoPrint 4000, a roll-fed, black and white printer, at a resolution of 600 dots per inch. 60lb offset, opaque, 480 PPI, crème white acid-free paper is used for the 6" x 9" trim sizes and smaller. The two larger sizes are printed on 50lb offset, opaque, 500 PPI, white acid-free paper.

Four-color covers for toExcel books are printed on the IBM InfoColor 70, which creates covers on quality white, 80-lb offset, enamel paper using a direct-to-paper, dry-toner technology. The printer is capable of producing an effective image resolution of 2,400 dots per inch—nearly indiscernible form offset quality. Covers are laminated.

Since toExcel uses the InfoColor 70, a four-color digital printer, we can produce a four-color cover for every book. Publishers who use traditional offset printing methods have to pay extra money for every color they use on a cover. Often, in order to save money, many publishers design covers using only black and one or two other colors. With digital printing, however, four-color color covers don't cost much more than black and white covers. This means that toExcel's professional cover designers can use the entire spectrum of four-color processing for every cover design.

After printing, the book block is married with its cover and perfect bound. It is now ready to be shipped to the customer.

Book selling

Our Web site, www.toExcel.com, is designed to simulate the traditional bookstore experience as much as possible. Visitors to the site can search for books by genre, such as fiction, poetry, biographies, and politics, or by using keywords associated with a book.

Once you find a book you're interested in, you can read a summary of the book and a profile of the author. You can even read the actual book, in its entirety, just as you could at a traditional bookstore. The "pages" of each toExcel book are viewable as low-resolution files, so that you can truly "try it before you buy it," a technique known to promote book sales.

Once you've decided to buy, you just fill out a simple form—like ordering from any of the online booksellers—and the book is printed and delivered to you. Online ordering will allow toExcel to set up a worldwide publishing network, so that any book available in the United States can also be bought in England, China, or Nigeria. In time, any book available in England, China, or Nigeria can be made available to buyers in the U.S. American authors will have the opportunity to reach a much larger audience, and American book buyers will have a much larger selection of books from which to choose—a special benefit for readers who want books written in their non-English native tongue and for researchers who want to learn more about a particular country's literature and culture.

Finally, once a book buying decision has been made at *toExcel.com*, customers pay for their purchase using toExcel's secure e-commerce system, which includes a range of shipping choices.

As a result of our strategic partnership with America's largest book distributor, Ingram Book Company, all toExcel books are added to the Ingram database, the most comprehensive in the industry. This allows all of our books to be available for purchase at traditional bookstores and other online book retailers by simply ordering via the book's ISBN.

An integral part of selling books on the Web is the ability to connect with your audience. toExcel uses the latest Web technologies, including free author and publisher Web pages, Web e-mail, message boards, the personalized "reading list" for members, ordering history, ability to change passwords, and numerous links to publishing, writing and other educational resources.

The exciting combination of design, print, marketing and commerce technologies that make toExcel's Open Publishing Platform™ unique means that no book need ever go out-of-print again. Researchers will always have access to any book they need, authors will never have to watch their work die a premature literary death, and international, niche and other titles of value can remain available.

The economic case

The bizarre economics of traditional printing are confusing. Publishers have to be able to balance the massive up-front costs of printing with the demand for a unique product, since every book title is a unique product. Add the costs of shipping, warehousing, and processing returned books, and it's easy to see that traditional publishers have a tough task balancing the bottom line.

There are over 25,000 book publishers in the United States. But few of these publishers have more than a handful of books in print at any one time. They can't afford to. The costs to set up a book, print it, market it, warehouse it, and ship it to bookstores across the continent prohibit most publishers from publishing as many books as they would like to.

Their economic troubles are the reason so many authors can't get published. After all, to justify the cost of an offset press run, publishers must be sure they can sell several thousand copies of a book. But does a book need to come with a guarantee that it will sell thousands of copies to make it worth publication?

By changing the way books are printed, sold and marketed, on-demand publishing is radically changing the economics of the publishing industry. Books with only a tiny potential readership will not only be feasible to publish, they will be profitable to publish for both author and publisher.

One reason for this radical economic change is the difference between the cost structures of traditional offset printing and digital printing. Offset printing involves large costs to make negatives and plates from which to print. Added to these costs is the time it takes to get an offset printing press ready for a new book. Because of these economic realities, publishers using offset printing methods must print hundreds or thousands of copies of each title at a time to be efficient. But printing all those books at once, before anyone has bought a single copy, means massive shipping and warehousing costs. And it often means that too many books are printed. Up to forty percent of the books are returned from bookstores unsold.

Is it any wonder traditional publishers can't afford to put more books into print?

Digital printing not only offers lower setup costs than offset printing, all of its costs are "one-time only." So, it costs the same to print 300 books at one time as it does to print 300 books over five years. The difference is huge. We print the books only as they are needed, we do away with warehousing costs and eliminate the problem of processing returned books altogether.

On-demand versus vanity publishing

The toExcel Open Publishing Platform™ relies on a sound new economic model that can be distinguished from traditional publishing as we've seen above. It can also be distinguished from traditional vanity publishing. toExcel is not the only publisher to promise aspiring authors a publishing platform. However, this is the first time an author who can't get a traditional publisher can publish his own work without incurring large costs and financial risk.

Vanity publishers of old promised—and still promise—to publish the work of any author willing to pay the setup and printing costs for his book. Since the offset printing process is expensive, clients of vanity presses have to pay thousands of dollars to finance a run of a few hundred copies. And sadly, the smaller the quantity, the higher the price per book. What's more, authors have to find a place to store the hundreds of books while they look for a way to sell them. Expensive? Yes. Why should a writer who has spent months or years researching and writing a book have to go into debt to publish it?

But many authors have published this way. And more than a few have been successful. For example, Jane Austen paid for the publication of *Mansfield Park*. Charles Dickens financed the publication of *A Christmas Carol*. J.R.R. Tolkein had to guarantee the publication costs of *The Lord of the Rings*, and more recently, Jill Paton Walsh, after fourteen rejections by commercial publishers, had to start her own publishing company to produce her 1994 Booker Prize-winning *Knowledge of Angels*.

But, these are the exceptions to the rule. Most vanity press books don't make a profit. How could they? Most aren't professionally designed, and are given no marketing support by their vanity publishers. You can't order them in traditional bookstores or through online booksellers, and the authors have very limited resources to get their marketing message out.

In spite of these facts, many vanity publishers continue to take advantage of those with "the dream" of publishing. But they really aren't fulfilling authors' dreams—after all, aspiring authors don't dream of a garage full of unsold books and a stifling level of debt. But that's what many get and it's a situation that has given vanity publishers a very bad name. Just search the topic on the Internet, and you will find a few publishers advertising for manuscripts along with several dozen warnings from the Better Business Bureau about vanity publishing scams.

Thanks to the new economics of publishing, and the extra services available from toExcel publishing, no author need ever again be ripped off just to make his or her dream come true. toExcel will publish almost any book for $299. For that publishing fee, an author's book is professionally designed with a four-color cover. The author gets three free copies of the book to give to family, friends or to send to interested book reviewers. Out-of print authors and publishers with titles they want to republish can also rely on toExcel's Open Publishing Platform™.

Each toExcel book is advertised and available for sale on our Web site and via other online and traditional booksellers. Web marketing tools are also provided to help promote sales. Authors and publishers are paid top royalties for every copy of their book sold.

toExcel takes care of all the essential paperwork necessary for publication, such as getting an ISBN number, and authors and publishers retain all copyrights to their book. toExcel books stay in print forever in a digital repository waiting to be printed on demand. Authors don't have to deal with a garage full of books they can't sell, and publishers have no inventory costs. That's the new economics of open publishing.

The product of the equation

toExcel Open Publishing Platform™, the industry's new paradigm, is based on a simple equation:

new technology + new economics = new opportunities.

On-demand publishing with toExcel is defined as cutting-edge technologies employed to create new economies that benefit author, publisher and reader. On-demand publishing is not only faster than traditional publishing, in which some books take up to eighteen months to get into print, it's less expensive in both time and money. The results are tremendous—a book that can never be out-of-print and opportunities that have never before existed.

The equation is egalitarian. It has created new opportunities for everyone:

- Opportunities for university presses to profitably publish and keep books in print.

- Opportunities for traditional publishers to explore and open new markets.

- Opportunities for authors to market and sell their work to a global audience.

- Opportunities for readers around the world to access out-of-print, hard-to-find, or previously unpublishable titles.

- Opportunities for direct communication, even collaboration, among readers, educators, knowledge experts, and authors.

Each of these opportunities is made possible by toExcel and on-demand publishing.

"I believe that toExcel's publishing effort reflects positively on me as an author who cares about his readers."

Danny Goodman, author
Danny Goodman's AppleScript™ Handbook

Chapter 3

Publishing with toExcel

What do Danny Goodman, Apple guru; Alan Simpson, software expert; Robert Rimmer, '60s erotica pioneer; Scott Stone, award-winning novelist; Crawford Kilian, sci-fi master; and Col. John Warden, architect of the air campaign that defeated Iraq in the Gulf War all have in common?

All have republished their out-of-print books with toExcel.

The technologies toExcel makes available for creating perfect digital files from existing books, make toExcel's Open Publishing Platform™ the perfect choice for republishing existing books of several types. Authors with out-of-print titles, international publishers, university presses and traditional publishers can all use toExcel to broaden their markets and distribution and better serve their customers.

OP authors return to their public

toExcel is uniquely suited for republishing out-of-print books, the rights to which have reverted to the author, and giving them new life. While some books about technology or science may become obsolete with time, many books are still as worthwhile a read today as they were the day they were published. But nobody is reading them today, because they aren't available.

Or at least they weren't. toExcel aims to bring as many out-of-print, out-of-stock books back to life as possible. Why should a good romance novel from the '70s be lost to the world just because it isn't a best seller anymore? A good story, with a strong plot and interesting characters is still a good read, even if the characters talk oddly and dress a little funny. A "groovy" book from the '70s is still a good book today.

That's why authors like Robert Rimmer are bringing their books back to life through toExcel. Mr. Rimmer sold millions of copies of his  books during the 60s and 70s, but only one of his novels, *The Harrad Experiment*, is still in print. Until he signed on with toExcel, his other novels were nearly impossible to find. Now all of his novels are available to anyone who wants them, and can be bought over the Web from almost anywhere on Earth.

He was even able to add a new preface to each of his books to put them in context for the '90s.

No wonder other authors are joining Mr. Rimmer and having all of their works brought back to life by toExcel. Their books are back in print and on sale, and they can start earning new royalties off of their past work. A great return for very little effort or expense.

Not everyone is using Windows™ 98. Lots of people are still in Win 95 and wanting *Alan Simpson's Easy Guide to Windows 95*. When  several of this best-selling author's titles went out-of-print, the rights to the text reverted to him. What better way to return the book to his loyal readers than to republish with toExcel. Our designers created a new cover, and now the book is available for all those who aren't quite ready to make the leap to Windows™ '98.

Simpson's books have been published throughout the world in dozens of languages and have sold millions of copies. toExcel has also republished his *WordPerfect® 6.1 for Windows™ Instant Reference, Understanding dBASE® 5 for Windows™, DOS® 6 Running Start, The ABC's of Quattro® Pro for Windows™,* and *Mastering WordPerfect® 6 for DOS.*

Scott Stone's *The Dragon's Eye* won the 1969 Edgar Award, given by the Mystery Writers Association of America. Why should this terrific novel be out-of-print? toExcel has republished this and Stone's other novels including *Spies*, *Song of the Wolf*, and *The Coasts of War*, which was the first full-length novel about American fighting in Vietnam.

Canadian novelist Crawford Kilian put in thousands of hours learning everything he could from a variety of resources about  Antarctica and its denizens in order to write his disaster epic *Icequake*. He estimates that he spent six to eight months "getting it right."

Out-of-print for years, *Icequake* is now back along with *Tsunami*, which was a groundbreaking page-turner in the realm of speculative science fiction.

Kilian has republished his '80s masterpieces *The Fall of the Republic*, *The Rogue Emperor*, and *The Empire of Time* (The Chronoplane Wars Trilogy) as well as *Gryphon*, and *Eyas*.

When you've got to win a war fast...
"The Air Force staff quickly came up with an air campaign, the brainchild of Colonel John Warden, a brilliant, brash fighter pilot and a leading 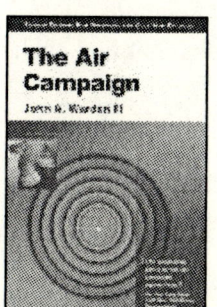 Air Force intellectual on the use of airpower...Warden's original plan would undergo numerous modifications...but his original concept remained the heart of the Desert Storm air war."

Colin Powell
Colin Powell, My American Journey

During the recent tension in Iraq, tacticians were clamoring for Warden's, The Air Campaign, long out-of-print. Col. Warden responded with a new edition published by toExcel to which a new preface and epilogue were added. Recommended by General Norman Schwarzkopf, this work of military strategy was republished by toExcel in less than eight weeks.

Linda Berman and Mary Ellen Siegel are professional psychotherapists experienced in the treatment of compulsive gambling. Before going out-of-print, this important book helped hundreds of spouses, parents, siblings, children, friends, and coworkers of problem gamblers. toExcel has recently brought this excellent book back in an updated 1999 edition to those who so desperately need it.

Jim Meade is president of Meade Ink, Inc., a writing services company, and is a consultant to Lotus, MCI, and many others. Meade is a best selling author of many computer books. His out-of-print titles, *PC Housekeeping: Maximizing Your PC* and *Power Excel for Windows® 95* are now republished by toExcel.

Case study: Danny Goodman

As we've seen, toExcel's Open Publishing Platform™ is an ideal choice for authors whose works are out-of-print yet have a modest demand. The perfect match of book and author came about when toExcel contacted Macintosh guru Danny Goodman about republishing two of his classics: *Danny Goodman's AppleScript™ Handbook* and *The Complete HyperCard 2.2 Handbook*, best-selling books that had each been out-of-print for more than five years.

Describing his decision to bring his books back into print with toExcel, Goodman stated:

> When I learned that toExcel could print on demand, book-length documents cost-effectively with such high quality, I knew I had found the solution for so many potential readers who could no longer locate copies of these out-of-print and

out-of-stock titles. It is also very gratifying that these books continue to be highly recommended, especially as Macintosh popularity rises again.

The response to early news of the republication was instantaneous. A man from Switzerland sent an e-mail message with the subject, "urgent! urgent!" and proclaimed, "for years, the Apple Community has waited for a reprint of Danny Goodman's *The Complete HyperCard 2.2 Handbook*. I heard that you are preparing this long-awaited reprint. Please drop me a note when it is finished—I will buy it at almost any cost."

Another Goodman fan gushed about *Danny Goodman's AppleScript™ Handbook* when he e-mailed, "Congratulations on deciding to publish *Danny Goodman's AppleScript™ Handbook*. You cannot get it published soon enough. There have been no serious competitors to Danny's book, and many newcomers to AppleScript desperately need a reference. Danny's is always quoted as being the best, but 'out-of-print'."

Even the editors at toExcel were quite surprised at the outpouring of enthusiasm, as there had only been a minimal amount of pre-publication marketing for the book. Suddenly a deluge of interest emerged—mostly through word-of-mouth in the wired AppleScript and HyperCard communities.

Goodman has helped demonstrate the power of the Web for authors by creating a robust Web page, **www.dannyg.com**, where he promotes all of his titles, both in-print and what were out-of-print. "My Web site is primarily a before-and after-sale information site for my books. For each of my books, I try to find out where the popular Web sites, newsgroups, and listservs are for the subject area. Gradually and politely, I try to make sure that my Web site becomes one of the destinations from these locations when someone is interested in a book on the subject."

This is a tremendous way in which to spur buyers. We asked Goodman a few questions about how to maximize his sales success with toExcel.

toExcel: Do you have any suggestions for how authors might better market their material electronically in order to gain the most from the toExcel publication? Do you use any others means, such as an e-mail newsletter, or listserv, to generate interest in your site and your books?

Goodman: It's important in the newsgroup and listserv arena to become a contributor to the community so that potential readers know you are listening to what's going on in the subject area. Most book authors try to hide from readers, but if you conduct yourself professionally and in a friendly, helpful manner in newsgroups and listservs, you will gain a lot of respect from people who are the influencers in that subject area. Rather than put blatant advertisements about my books in these messages, I simply add the title and my Web site URL to the signature line for each message. If you can add further value to your own Web site, such as live examples or downloadable example files, you can also apply for inclusion in the popular Web search engines, such as Yahoo and AltaVista. This is a lengthy process, but a combination of patience and persistence can pay off.

toExcel: What benefits have you seen from the toExcel program?

Goodman: Initially toExcel was able to satisfy pent-up demand for two out-of-print titles. Now that the titles are readily available, I find that active members in the online communities of those subject areas (in newsgroups and listservs) recommend the titles to newcomers looking for books. I have an army of salespeople on the Internet, most of whom I've never met.

toExcel: Do you see this as a way to promote your in-print books?

Goodman: I believe that toExcel's publishing effort reflects positively on me as an author who cares about his readers. This can only direct those readers to my in-print titles in the future if their work or studies take them in the direction of those titles.

toExcel: Does the availability of your toExcel titles in full-text versions online help or hinder sales?

Goodman: Even though the Adobe Acrobat files are nice to look at, I believe it is very inconvenient to read a book-length document on a computer screen. Having the full text online is akin to letting a potential reader browse through the book at the bookstore. A selected excerpt will likely not have a representative sample of information the reader is looking for. There may be some who refer to the book only in its online version, or spend even more money to print out the Acrobat files themselves, but they are also probably not ones who would buy a book in any case. In my opinion, the online version only helps sales of the printed copies.

These published authors have taken advantage of the opportunities created by new technology and new economics, the opportunity we call toExcel's Open Publishing Platform™. You can, too.

International publishers open new markets

Authors of out-of-print books are not the only ones who can benefit from partnering with toExcel. International publishers can benefit, too.

There are more than 30 million Spanish speakers in the United States alone. French is one of two languages commonly taught in the United States school system. There is a large Japanese expatriate community in the United States and Canada. So, where do these readers buy books in Spanish, French, and Japanese? There are no book superstores, no bookstore Web sites, and few Mom and Pop booksellers selling to the non-English-speaking populations in North America. The market is huge. No one has taken advantage of this potential, this pent-up demand, until toExcel.

International publishers can now use toExcel's turnkey production, printing, and distribution system like a factory to get non-English titles to the North American market faster, cheaper, and with less risk than they could any other way. This leaves international publishers free to focus on the smart work of publishing, like title acquisition, while toExcel takes care of the production and distribution infrastructure.

International publishers can revive out-of-print books, in-print titles or even new titles to the North American market, gaining instant distribution online and in bookstores, while significantly reducing costs and risks.

toExcel makes it easy and inexpensive to expand revenues in this way. Partnering with toExcel helps international publishers reach new audiences without the difficulty and expense of creating a new distribution channel. toExcel offers new revenue without new costs...a new source of profits.

On-demand publishing opens the North American book market to foreign language books on a larger scale than was ever dreamed possible before. North America, more than any other place on Earth, is a melting pot of people from different countries and ethnic backgrounds. While many of the larger ethnic groups have access to books in their own language, they have a very limited selection compared to their English speaking neighbors, who browse at both traditional and online bookstores.

While limited selection made sense a decade ago, there is no longer any reason why a Chinese woman living in Kansas shouldn't have quick access to hundreds if not thousands of books written in Mandarin. And not just old, classic titles, but the latest works of China's newest voices as well. This is all possible now through on-demand publishing. toExcel is leading the way in bringing foreign language books to the American market.

In 1999, toExcel published books in several languages, including Chinese, Japanese, French, and Spanish. We are working aggressively to make partners and acquire foreign-language titles so we can provide the North American market with the selection it deserves.

As our global publishing network grows, borders will no longer play a big role in the publishing world. A novel published in Russia will be available in the U.S., France, England or Yemen. And why shouldn't it be? New ideas and great stories shouldn't be constrained by geography. Not when we have the technology to electronically link the entire world.

Case studies: Éditions du Rocher and Tachibana Publishing Group

Éditions du Rocher is a large French publisher of such literary giants as Rimbaud and Cocteau. Working with toExcel, Éditions du Rocher has published its highly acclaimed titles in the U.S. for the first time in French. toExcel published over forty Éditions du Rocher titles in the first quarter of 1999.

Titles were selected by both companies to cater to the American school system's French classes and the general French-speaking population in the United States. Cocteau, author of *La Belle et la bête* or *Beauty and the Beast*, was selected for its potential interest to the American school system.

French novels by new authors such as Shan Sa (*Porte de la Paix céleste*), winner of the prestigious Prix Goncourt, were selected for their appeal to native French readers. Other highly esteemed authors include Claude Mourthé, Gerard de Nerval, and Jean Giono.

Tachibana Publishing Group is an incredibly successful publisher of New Age and other Japanese-language books whose titles often sell into the hundreds of thousands in Japan. toExcel is publishing Tachibana's books in North America to support the publisher in its mission to serve the large Japanese expatriate population in the U.S. and Canada. Over fifty titles have already been republished. The Japanese population will be contacted through targeted advertising to Japanese Web sites and community groups throughout North America.

In addition to catering to the American school system and non-English speaking populations in North America, toExcel will select titles appealing to the American public library system. Public libraries are obligated to carry books in languages that reflect the populations those libraries serve. Thus, as non-English speaking populations increase in North America, the number and diversity of books carried by libraries in those languages will also increase.

Because of toExcel's early agreements with Tachibana and Éditions du Rocher, these two forward-looking publishers will be the first featured in toExcel's non-English language book selling center at www.toExcel.com. toExcel intends to become the North American center for publishing and selling books to the Spanish, French, Japanese, Chinese, German and Italian-speaking population in North America.

University presses in the vanguard

toExcel's Open Publishing Platform™ helps university presses better serve the publishing needs of the university, its professors, and graduate students. University presses have long struggled with a challenging dilemma—how to balance the desire to publish and keep in print diverse intellectual content with the economic realities of traditional publishing.

toExcel, the industry leader of a new breed of publisher, has opened a new world of publishing opportunity for university presses. By combining the latest in digital "on-demand" printing technologies with the marketing and sales power of the Internet, toExcel enables university presses to profitably publish and market low-demand titles, specialty books, or publications with narrow academic appeal.

By helping to create incremental revenue without incremental headache, toExcel helps university presses overcome the bottom-line realities imposed on their operations. Academic presses can offer better service and make more net revenue with no more net effort. And they can even extend their reach into new markets or imprints with little additional risk.

toExcel's Open Publishing Platform™ is a unique resource that allows university presses to:

- Better balance their academic interests with their economic concerns.
- Publish any book economically, even low-demand or niche titles.
- Republish out-of-print books at no cost, at no risk.
- Keep good intellectual content in-print forever, without concern for economics.

- Have a resource to market and test-market books to a wide audience.
- Create a "win-win" situation for the university community.

Professors and graduate students win because the university press can afford to publish every manuscript it develops. Academics get to publish, not perish. The press wins because it offers better service and creates a new source of revenue.

Case studies: Harvard and Columbia universities

Institutions like Harvard University Press and Columbia University Press see a toExcel partnership as a winning proposition. toExcel's  work with these university presses in particular, highlights how a combination of on-demand printing and Internet distribution can prolong the life of a particular title's revenue stream far past the point of what was possible with traditional publishing methods.

toExcel believes that this revenue stream is significant if a large number of titles from a variety of university presses can be collected and sold by one entity. toExcel's work with Harvard University Press and Columbia University Press represents toExcel's initial efforts to take advantage of this opportunity.

On-demand printing allows toExcel to inexpensively publish "low-demand books," such as Harvard University Press or Columbia University Press titles. Because toExcel prints the books one-at-a-time upon customer request, there is no guessing, as in traditional publishing, as to the number of books to print to fulfill demand. True demand for a title determines supply. Titles like Columbia's *Just Before the Origin* can be brought back to the academic community and be available to the scholars and researchers who need them.

Since many members of academia and others interested in specialty titles are "Web-savvy," Internet marketing is a force for raising demand for niche market books. For example, toExcel recently republished an out-of-print title, *The Airline Pilots,* which reviews the history of the unionization of airlines, for Harvard University Press. Airline pilot

associations, airplane Web sites and aviation aficionados were contacted about the availability of the book, drawing customers to toExcel's retail Web site. Internet marketing has proven very effective in selling niche market books to niche communities.

toExcel's publishing agreements with Columbia University Press and Harvard University Press, two of the most prestigious academic publishing establishments in the world, help promote important academic work by the most important scholars of the past and present. If knowledge is power, toExcel's efforts with university presses aims to distribute that power "one book at a time."

toExcel expects to increase its scope into the university press market to become the destination on the Internet for formerly out-of-print university press books.

Note: toExcel can also support individual educators, researchers, independent academics, or institutions that don't have a formal press. See Chapter 4.

Traditional publishers get more books on the list

Publishers have long been forced to make acquisition decisions based on traditional publishing economics, not on intellectual content or meeting readers' needs. Even exceptional niche or high-potential experimental works have been denied a market.

Now, toExcel's Open Publishing Platform™ has opened the door to a new era of publishing opportunities. Beloved out-of-print titles, titles by new authors, specialty books...all can now be marketed to a wide audience, printed one-at-a-time as ordered, and delivered to the hands of readers. By combining the latest in digital on-demand printing technologies with the marketing and sales power of the Internet, toExcel enables traditional publishers to profitably market low-demand titles.

For the first time, publishers have the opportunity to tap into the potential profitability of low-demand titles. toExcel is a unique resource that allows traditional publishers to republish out-of-print books at no cost, at no risk; publish and market any book economically, even low-demand or niche titles; test market new or experimental books inexpensively and to a wide audience; and keep titles with low but continual demand in print, reaping the economic benefits of ongoing sales.

While publishers previously have had access to on-demand printing, they were often thwarted by the high cost of digital pre-press and the challenges of low-volume distribution. toExcel has overcome these obstacles, providing publishers with a turnkey system to digitally pre-press, market, print, and distribute books one-at-a-time, with exceptional quality, speed, and competitive pricing.

The advantages for publishers are considerable. Existing books are scanned and digitally formatted for on-demand printing. toExcel provides this turnkey pre-press at no charge to publishers. toExcel's online bookstore lets publishers reach, market, and sell titles to diverse audiences. The Internet is an easy way to test new titles or build interest and demand for books that publishers are considering producing traditionally. toExcel eliminates the need to build and maintain your own commerce-enabled Web site.

toExcel offers free Web homepages and message boards to publishers so titles can be promoted and marketed in the way they want...at very little cost. Printing quality is identical to traditionally printed soft-cover books, including full-color laminated covers. Books are priced comparably to standard soft-cover books, and publishers retain copyright/imprint rights, so books can be moved to traditional publishing at any time.

Partnering with toExcel is a way for traditional full-line publishers to increase revenue without risk by reviving out-of print titles, keeping books in print, and through economical online viewing and on-demand printing. toExcel helps publishers expand their lines of available books and customized publications without incurring the costs and risks associated with short-run printing.

Case study: The Coriolis Group

toExcel has recently entered into an agreement with The Coriolis Group to republish several out-of-print computer titles from its Ventana imprint including *Object-Oriented Programming in Java 1.1, Online Guide to Medical Research, The Comprehensive Guide to Microsoft*

Office 97, and *The Visual Basic Programmer's Guide to Java*.

This agreement marks another step in toExcel's efforts to put out-of-print computer books back into the user's hands. The books will be available at toExcel's online bookstore and through toExcel's distributor, Ingram Books, in Spring '99.

Specialty publishers can reap the same benefits toExcel offers to major imprints. Technical and scientific publishers for example can expand their publishing base without expanding the amount of work it takes to serve their audiences. The same incremental revenue without incremental risk results from producing, printing and distributing books one-at-a-time. Specialty publishers can better serve their loyal readers, while simplifying the way they do business. They can increase their offerings within their core areas while extending their presses into new markets or imprints with little additional risk.

Businesses and organizations can also get all the benefits mentioned above, plus, they get the flexibility and variable cost advantages of outsourcing an area that is not a core competency. By publishing documentation, employee manuals, reports, government filings, etc. in book form one-at-a-time on demand, employees, partners, and customers are better served, and inventory, space, and administration costs are eliminated.

toExcel publishing partners

Some of the very first toExcel partners include:

>Fudan University (Shanghai, China)
>
>East China Normal University (Shanghai, China)
>
>Columbia University Press
>
>Harvard University Press
>
>University of Nebraska–Lincoln Division of Continuing Studies
>
>The Coriolis Group
>
>Tachibana

Jones and Bartlett
Alan Simpson
Martin Rinehart
Douglas J. Wolf
Anthony Alessandra
James Cathcart
Phillip Wexler
Linda Berman
Mary Ellen Siegel
Clarke Wallace
Col. John A. Warden III, USAF
Crawford Kilian
Daniel J. Nassar
Danny Goodman
David Hapgood
David Loye
David W. Kirkpatrick
Douglas K. Smith
Robert C. Alexander
George Cohen
James G. Meade
Jeffery Young
John Selby-Smith
L.E. Ward
Louis Untermeyer
Michael J. Driver
Kenneth R. Brousseau
Phillip L. Hunsaker
Randy Harris

Raymond Trevor Bradley
Renaldo Fischer, M.D
Michele St. George
Riane Tennenhaus Eisler
Robert Rimmer
Scott C.S. Stone
Tomás González

"The cover design is awesome. Fiery and bold. I am very pleased. The photo insertion is perfect."

"The formatting is just lovely, beautiful. I went through the pages with goose bumps. It's really coming into life. Wonderful. Thank you very much."

Renaldo Fischer, M.D., author
Mystics in the Street

Chapter 4

A New Way to Get Published

Whether you realize it or not, you know someone who has "the dream."

A trial lawyer in Miami who wants to be the next John Grisham. A retired cop in Toronto who thinks his memoirs could be a best seller. An English professor in London who wants to write a book on her latest research on Shakespeare's political views. An investment banker in New York who wants to write the ultimate investment guide. A grandmother in Perth who pictures herself as an Australian Agatha Christie. All longing to get published. toExcel can make "the dream" come true for you.

For individual authors and anyone else tired of submitting a manuscript over the transom and waiting months for a reply, toExcel opens up a new world of possibilities with The People's Press—toExcel's tool to help new author's get their books into print. We use our Open Publishing Platform™ to publish your manuscript in a bookstore quality paper, perfect-bound format with a custom, eye-catching, four-color cover.

There are many good reasons to choose toExcel to publish your manuscript:

No rejection letters from The People's Press

It's easy. You submit your manuscript. We do the pre-press work to turn it into a bookstore-quality book, make it readable and sellable on our Web site and through traditional bookstores and on-line bookstores. We register your ISBN number, give you Web tools to promote and sell your book, and send you three finished copies.

It's fast. We go from your manuscript to best-seller-quality book, ready to sell anywhere in a few weeks, or less. Traditional publishers regularly take over a year to put a manuscript into print.

It's inexpensive. For only $299, you're published. No rejections. Your ideas are made available to the world immediately in leading traditional bookstores, online bookstores, and on our Web site.

It's real. toExcel is not a slick marketing gimmick nor a vanity press. What you see is what you get. We've developed the world's first Open Publishing Platform™ that changes the fundamental economics of publishing, much like the assembly line did for Ford. It's being used by prestigious university presses like Harvard and Columbia to print and distribute books efficiently, one-at-a-time. In effect, toExcel is the world's first online book factory.

It's unlimited. Using our state-of-the-art technology and distribution network (including a strategic partnership with Ingram—the world's biggest book distributor—and its Lightning Print division), your book can be printed and shipped automatically, one-at-a-time, anywhere in the world. You retain the copyright, so if you want to publish it somewhere else, you can. We can print your book in volume for you. We can print customized or gift versions for you. We will help you to sell it using Internet technology and marketing tools. Yet you always have total flexibility and total control.

It's successful. Previously published authors like William Gladstone, Robert Rimmer and Renaldo Fischer have chosen to publish their new manuscripts with toExcel. And new first-time authors are joining us every day.

Marketing your book

Like any other publisher, toExcel uses its own sales and marketing judgement and expertise in making advertising and promotional decisions. Nonetheless, every book published by toExcel is supported by a unique set of marketing tools and resources that are limited only by the creativity and energy of each author.

When you publish with toExcel, we give you a suite of Web-based tools that virtually ensure you'll sell enough books to pay back your initial modest investment, and more than likely, make money on your ideas. For starters, we host and help you create an author's page on our Web site where people can see a picture of you, and read your personal statements about your book and your background. Think of your author's page as a live, interactive version of the "about the author" page you see on all the bestsellers.

Next, you get an automated bulletin board or message board. This tool enables your readers to exchange comments on your book with other readers, and with you, in an open, freewheeling format for all to read and participate in. You'll create a community of interest around your book that jump-starts its "word-of-mouth" advertising, the most powerful marketing program in publishing.

You get our package of promotional secrets, tips, and links to important resources that tell you how to inform your local news media of your accomplishment, use the Web to spread the word (including example e-mail messages) and other proven success secrets of best-selling authors and publishers.

And finally, we make your book readable in its entirety online in our Readercentral.com Web site, which we call the world's largest reading room. Of course, readers can buy your book through the toExcel bookstore, as well. And we handle all order processing, printing, delivery and administration for you automatically. You simply sit back and collect the royalty checks.

With our support, you'll use the power of the Internet to become a successful author in a radically different and better way than the traditional publishing system. We provide the tools, but your possibilities are unlimited.

Case studies

New author **Duane Simolke** invites readers to visit the historical West Texas town of Acorn. Enjoy the German festival, a high school football game, homemade apple pie from the Turner Street Cafe, and the cool shade of a hundred-year-old oak tree. Just be careful, because in Acorn the sky is always falling.

Hoping to realize his dream and become a full-time writer, Duane Simolke chose to publish his first fiction collection, *The Acorn Stories*, with toExcel. With a passion for creating and a lifetime dedicated to the written word, Duane brings alive the town of Acorn, Texas.

As a young boy in Louisiana, Duane knew he would be a writer. From creating additional scenarios about his favorite comic book or Star Trek characters to penning fresh lyrics to his favorite songs, Duane felt a need to get his thoughts out on paper. His vivid imagination soon had him writing original poems and song lyrics, and he began writing his first novel *(Degranon)* at fifteen. It was clear to all that knew him that Duane was determined to see his ideas in print.

Duane is excited about his partnership with toExcel and has future works in progress. When asked why he chose toExcel, he responded, "It just seemed like an obvious way to get my book to a large audience—anyone can order it from a bookstore and it's never going to go out-of-print." What could be better for any new author?

Ron Gilster and colleagues Connie Gleason and Joe Bush are the core of the Communication Technology Center at Walla Walla Community College in Walla Walla, Washington.

Like most teachers, they wanted unique teaching materials tailored to their own students' needs. Although they had published traditionally (an earlier edition of their new toExcel book called *Passport to Information Literacy* was published by McGraw-Hill), they wanted a fast, no-hassle edition for their Fall '98 classes. The manuscript was sent to toExcel in MS Word® with the screen shots and other graphics embedded in the file. Within weeks the book was available to students from the toExcel site, as well as from the school bookstore.

When you've got a passion for the stage, you've just got to pursue it! toExcel author **Bea Fogelman**, mother of acclaimed celebrity impersonator Sherie Rae, is one stage-struck senior and a terrific writer as

well. A long-time resident of Las Vegas, Bea knew early on that she had a very talented daughter. Sherri made her first professional recording at 14, and was tapped for *Legends in Concert* as Janis Joplin before she finished college.

Now, Bea has tapped into her unique backstage access to tell the stories of the fascinating folk who choose to hide their own personalities and take on those of the stars. In 1994, Bea started writing a short story about daughter Sherie Rae. Friends of Sherie's heard about the "work-in-progress" and began telling their own stories. *CopyCats* was born.

A Web-savvy writer with her own Web page, Bea took advantage of toExcel's People's Press to publish her labor of love. Bea has been very happy with the service provided by toExcel's People's Press. So much so that she's hard at work on her next book titled *The Filmakers*. A ball of fire, Bea is also working on a Broadway musical. And, when not working on her many writing projects, Bea and husband Leo, a pharmacist, enjoy their three children, seven grandchildren and three great-grandchildren.

Bea is thrilled to see her book for sale at *barnesandnoble.com* and *Amazon.com*, but she wisely directs buyers to the www.toexcel.com to buy the book directly from the publisher at a substantial discount. She's looking forward to her first royalty checks and to telling her friends online and off about being published by toExcel, the leader of the publishing revolution.

Born in the hill country of Texas and raised on the legends of Pecos Bill and Slue Foot Sue, storytelling just comes naturally to **Mike Danford**, former member of the "corporate bureaucracy."

In the spirit of the tall tales of early American folklore, comes Mike Danford's new book *No Sudden Moves!* That this story captures all the flavor of a yarn spun out while settin' on the front porch on a summer's eve is no surprise once you've spoken to the author. With a soft Texas drawl and a casual writing style born of a childhood filled with cowboys and cattle drives, Mike's first book is, literally, a dream come true.

During his tenure in the corporate world, Danford started writing parables for the company newsletter, some of which were later printed in the local newspapers. "A small following developed to the point that I was kinda surprised and even embarrassed when strangers in the grocery stores would talk to me like I was an old friend." After retiring early from his job, "because I felt I just had better things to do," this father of five began writing full time, turning a habit formed of his love of telling stories for the amusement of others into a new vocation.

This may be Danford's first book, but it certainly will not be his last. With *No Sudden Moves!* only just recently published, he has two more books nearly finished that he will publish with toExcel and the seeds of a fourth are germinating.

Miami-based writer **Wes Patterson** has enjoyed a lifetime of writing, creating and healing. With degrees in Creative Writing and Psychology from Johns Hopkins University and the University of Florida, the author fills his days with two of his greatest passions—writing and counseling. With the release of his first book, *Past the Galaxies of Stars*, Mr. Patterson makes his debut as a toExcel author.

Born and raised in Manhattan, Wes began writing short stories and poems around the age of ten. As a sophomore at Johns Hopkins, he received permission to take graduate courses in Creative Writing under the tutelage of Elliot Coleman. Furthering his education at the University of Florida, Wes continued to explore his potential, working with such notables as Smith Kirkpatrick and Frank Bush. Though the encouragement and insights of these professionals were invaluable to him, he also realizes he would be writing regardless. "I have always been very self-directed. I have always had a need to write and have felt very driven to do so. Everything just comes from within."

Wes credits his partnership with toExcel as a terrific "twist of fate." After countless queries and piles of rejection slips, Bill Gladstone, founder of Waterside Productions, came across one of the author's requests. Having successfully published his own new book with toExcel, Bill realized that another successful partnership could be formed and put Wes in touch with toExcel. The rest is history.

Wes is currently working on a novel entitled *Wherever You May Be Searching* and expects to have it completed in the next few months.

If you're ready to make "the dream" come true for you, as it has for these and other toExcel authors, read on.

How it works

Submitting a manuscript to toExcel is easy. Just follow the guidelines on our Web site to create your submission package. toExcel will take your manuscript, submitted in MS Word® or WordPerfect® format and turn it into a bookstore-quality book for you. Your book will be printed with a glossy, four-color laminated cover based on your design ideas and the ideas of our experienced book-cover designers. We format your manuscript for on-demand publishing and make it ready for order on our site or at any bookstore. We'll also make your book available for online reading on our ReaderCentral Web site. Once your book is finished, you get three finished copies automatically.

We obtain an ISBN number for you, and include your book in the Ingram Book database, making it available instantly by special order in virtually any traditional or online bookstore. With this powerful distribution alliance, you or your friends can walk into or call any bookstore and order your book by its ISBN number. Anywhere in the world. At any time.

toExcel provides you with Web marketing tools and helps you create your own author's Web site where anyone with Internet access can read your books in their entirety, correspond with you and your readers via e-mail and or discussion group, and buy your book through a secure transaction.

We make your book available to buy on-demand toll-free by phone and on the Web. Every time it's ordered, we print and ship it automatically within forty-eight hours of order. We handle all billing, administration, and collections, and pay you top royalties

You're done. You're ready to submit. After months of waking up at 5 A.M. to write a few pages before work, and giving up your weekends to finish a few more pages, you have finally completed the "great American novel." It's all ready to be published. Or is it?

Unlike other publishers, toExcel does not limit the number of titles it will publish. What this means is simple—you need to submit a *complete submission package* to toExcel and then we'll evaluate where your project stands.

First we'll need your signed agreement and payment. The latest version is available for download on our Web site or by contacting toExcel. Be sure to read all the provisions carefully and follow submission guidelines.

Second, we need a completed title submission form. Again, the latest version is available for download on our Web site or by contacting toExcel.

Whenever submitting to toExcel, authors should always be sure to use the appropriate and latest version of these two documents from our site. They are critical for the successful production of your book. The information you provide will include back cover copy for the book and information about creating the front cover.

The title submission form will also help us market your book. Please complete all of the sections as accurately and completely as possible. Keywords are an important means to help interested customers find your work on the Internet, and the marketing description and author bio you provide will be posted on the toExcel Web site.

Finally, we need you manuscript. You have complete responsibility for your final edited text manuscript, so you'll want to make sure the book is edited to the very highest standards it deserves. You will have several editorial-development options, which toExcel explains on its Web site.

Hemingway had an editor. Steinbeck had one. Everyone needs one. After months of writing, rewriting, and editing your work, you need a fresh set of eyes to look over your work. Make sure all the following sections are included in your manuscript and that the information on them is consistent.

Half-title page (required): We need the exact title of your book.

Title page (required): We need the exact title of your book, any subtitle, and your name as you wish it to appear everywhere in and on the book.

Copyright page (required): Make sure we have the correct name and spelling for the copyright holder (usually the author...your name as you wish it to appear everywhere in and on the book.) We also need information about any copyrighted information (graphics or text) you are reprinting with permission.

Dedication page (optional): Dedications are best kept short. It is not necessary to use the word dedication—To will usually do. You don't have to include the full name of the person you are dedicating the book to, or the life dates of a person who has died, although both are acceptable.

Epigraph page (optional): An epigraph is a pertinent quotation used at the beginning of the book. The source of the quote should be given in the line following the quotation. Only the author's name and the title of the work are needed. Page numbers and bibliographical details are not used.

Table of Contents page (optional): If you require a table of contents, please do not include page numbers. All we need are the items. After we lay out the text, we will assign the correct page numbers in the table of contents you have given us.

Foreword page (optional): A foreword is usually a short essay by someone other than the author or editor. Sometimes it is written by a well-known person whose name appears on the title page, for example, "With a Foreword by Richard Nixon."

Preface page (optional): A preface is the author's own statement about the work. A preface often includes reasons for writing the book and a discussion of research methods used.

Acknowledgements page (optional): Acknowledgments are used to thank everyone who helped make your book possible. They work best when they are brief.

Introduction page (optional): Unlike a preface, which is about the writing of the book, an introduction includes text relevant to the book's topic that should be read before reading the rest of the book. It could include historical information that puts the rest of your book into context. A long introduction or one that actually begins the subject of the text shouldn't be separated from the book. It should be used as the opening chapter.

Index pages (optional): toExcel cannot create a contextual index, but we can create a simple item index. Please do not include page numbers in your index. All we need are the exact text items as they are found in the body of your book. After we lay out the text, we will assign the correct page numbers to the index entries you have given us.

About the Author (optional): If you want a short bio of yourself at the back of the book, you need to write a brief piece explaining who you are. Remember, this bio is your way of letting the reader know what expertise you have to write this book—this is especially important for non-fiction writers. Insert this page at the end of your manuscript file. If you have a picture, please embed the digital file in the text.

For complete submission guidelines, please visit our Web site at www.toExcel.com or contact toExcel.

toExcel Authors

Bea Fogelman

Duane Simolke

Luther Butler

Michael Danford

Robert Rimmer

Ron Gilster

Wes Patterson

William Gladstone

Alex Siegel

Fritz Ringer

Mark A. Roeder

Michelle Harris
Renaldo Fischer
Katherine Minott
Steven Michael Daniel
Dana Barbour

"I've just gone through the HTML 4.0 Specifications book, the first in the Open Documents Standards Library series, and am mightily impressed. I see no reason why this book wouldn't do very well as a standard stock item in bookstores. It's every bit as good and thorough as an O'Reilly Nutshell book, and we know the authors are absolutely accurate, because they formalized the HTML 4.0 specs!"

Gordon McComb, computer book author and consultant

Chapter 5

toExcel's Own Book Series

There are numerous sources of valuable and important information and toExcel is striving to make that information available in book form to its readers.

The Open Documents and Open Source Libraries

The book you hold in your hand is an real-life example of toExcel's revolutionary Open Publishing Platform™. The Open Documents and Open Source Libraries are an extension of toExcel's mission, They are the product of a unique publishing initiative that brings important online and other documents to the public in printed form…quickly and efficiently.

toExcel is actively working with Web sites and other information providers to distribute information to the widest possible audience via our unique on-demand publishing technology. We are committed to bringing into print the titles the public needs and wants…from the works of the World Wide Web Consortium to the latest information from the open source movement. We get new and updated titles into the hands of the public fast. What's more, all toExcel book are always available to be read online, free at our site, in keeping with the core philosophy of the open documents movement.

Each title in toExcel's Open Documents and Open Source Libraries is a printed version of the latest industry-accepted specifications and contains the complete, unedited text of the original document. toExcel provides these books as a service to the developers' community for use as a timely and handy desktop companion, saving the reader the time and expense of printing the documentation.

Titles in the Open Documents and Open Source Libraries include:

    W3C: HTML 4.0 Specification

    W3C: HTML 3.2 Reference Specification

    W3C: Extensible Stylesheet Language (XSL)

    W3C: Extensible Markup Language (XML) 1.0 Specifications

    W3C: Document Object Model Specification, Level 1

    W3C: Document Object Model Specification, Level 2

    W3C: Cascading Style Sheets Specification, Level 1

    W3C: Cascading Style Sheets Specification, Level 2

    W3C: Synchronized Multimedia Integration Language (SMIL) 1.0 Specification

    W3C: Hypertext Transfer Protocol HTTP/1.0 Specifications

    W3C: Security, Privacy, and Content Rating: Application Notes

    W3C: Amaya Application Notes

    W3C: Hypertext Transfer Protocol HTTP/1.x Specifications

    W3C: Jigsaw Application Notes

    ECMA: Application Programming Interface for Windows

    ECMA: ECMAScript Language Specification

    AWK Language Programming: A User's Guide for GNU AWK

    Apache Administrator's Guide

    Apache Server Configuration and Runtime Directives

    The Power of Apache

    Apache Programmer's Guide

    Python Programming Manual

    PHP Programming Manual

    K Desktop

Linux Howto Collection: Linux Installation and Upgrade
Linux Howto Collection: Using Linux with Windows and DOS
Linux Howto Collection: Hardware Guide to Linux
Linux Howto Collection: Introduction Linux
Linux Howto Collection: Linux Modem and Serial Communications

The New Millennium Library

The New Millenium Library represents another important extension of toExcel's mission to distribute the great books of our civilization to the widest possible audience via free online viewing for everyone and perpetual availability through our unique on-demand publishing technology.

New Millennium Library editions are created by applying the information age's newest technologies to the most traditional artifact of modern civilization: the printed book.

The power of digital processing brings publishing into a new era, one in which the book, far from vanishing, becomes more available and more indispensable than ever. The New Millennium Library will make hundreds, eventually thousands, of books available at our Web site for free online browsing in attractively designed, easy-to-read formats. Most importantly, all titles can be printed, upon demand, as traditionally bound books. When you find a book you would like to own, all you have to do is order it.

Of course, these are not mere print-outs nor typewriter texts, but beautifully designed and sturdily bound paper back editions, just like the best literary and academic editions you buy at a bookstore. Our titles, however, are never out-of-stock and never go out-of-print.

In the New Millennium Library you will find an ever growing list of well-known "classics." You'll also find lesser-known treasures and hard-to-find popular works from the past that have frequently, until now, been difficult to make available to general readers.

Our first offerings, for example, range from Mark Twain's *The Adventures of Huckleberry Finn* to Sax Rohmer's, *The Insidious Dr. Fu-Manchu*. Contemporary introductions briefly situate each work in its historical context and explain its enduring pleasures and importance.

You may browse our online reading room, visiting often to watch our list of perennial favorites and nearly lost gems grow. You may collect these attractively bound editions to enjoy wherever and whenever you like. You may also offer suggestions for titles that you'd like to see added to the library.

The academic editors of our New Millennium Library series believe that the Internet is the future of publishing, and suddenly, for the book in the new millennium, everything is possible.

The Open Stories Series

Technology has helped make it possible for people to make their voices heard around the world on an unlimited number of topics. The World Wide Web—technology's answer to the soapbox of old—has provided a way for regular people to tell their stories and make their voices heard to an audience they could have never dreamed of reaching before. But the abundance of chat rooms and message boards that have popped up all over the Web don't offer any permanence. The views and stories that are written in these rooms often disappear almost as quickly as they are written.

toExcel takes this concept one step further. We have set up space on our Web site to collect stories and essays from regular people on a host of different topics. Stories and ideas that will not only be available all over the world, but will be available years from now for anyone interested in learning how real people felt about the issues and events of today.

Anyone can pick up a textbook and find out how the top opinion makers of the late '90s reacted to the impeachment of Bill Clinton, but will the real emotions and concerns of everyday American be available to researchers in the future. These opinions are being collected on the Web, but most of these collections won't last—the Web is not a well-archived source of information. toExcel will change that.

Our editors will collect all of the submissions to one of the many topics we will open for discussion, choose the best ones, and compile them into a book. If your submission is selected, we'll print your name and bio in the book and give you two free copies. These Open Stories books will be sold on our site and at traditional and online bookstores.

In the coming months, we'll be accepting submissions for different categories of interest. We'll have categories like religious/faith anecdotes, war stories, investment tips, workplace horror stories, and many more.

Currently toExcel is collecting essays for three books at our main Web site, www.toExcel.com. The books deal with three diverse topics. The first, *We the People*, is a collection of essays about peoples' reactions to and thoughts about the Monica Lewinsky scandal and the impeachment of President Bill Clinton. The second book, *True Love*, is a collection of stories of romance and communion that make the soul sing. Finally, third book is a collection of inspirational stories written by everyday people.

Feel free to drop by our Web site to write your own essay or story on one of these topics or to see what new topics we have started collecting essays for.

The edUniverse–University of Nebraska–Lincoln Learning Series

toExcel and its educational Web site, edUniverse, are partnering with the University of Nebraska–Lincoln to create excellent self-study courses based on the accredited, award-winning curriculum of its Independent Study High School, a part of the Division of Continuing Studies.

Founded in 1929, the University of Nebraska–Lincoln Independent Study High School serves nearly 14,000 enrollments annually from all 50 states of the United States and more than 135 other countries. The ISHS has produced seven National Merit scholars in the past six years.

The UNL Independent Study High School is fully accredited by the North Central Association of Colleges and Schools and the Nebraska Department of Education. As such it grants hundreds of course credits and diplomas each year.

UNL courses have won more national awards for course excellence than any other institution. The University Continuing Education Association (UCEA) has honored this curriculum with over 50 awards...at least one each year since 1976.

Never before has this award-winning curriculum been available to be printed one-at-a-time, on-demand for the general public. With toExcel's revolutionary Open Publishing Platform™, these course books can be produced, marketed, and distributed on-demand...one-at-a-time.

There are twenty-two courses in the edUniverse-University of Nebraska–Lincoln Learning Series. Each course is derived from the curriculum of the University of Nebraska–Lincoln Independent Study High School and is appropriate for anyone who wants to review and improve his or her skills in basic high school grammar and math. This series marries education's proven tool—the self-study workbook—with the exciting power of the Internet. Users get traditional distance education plus online tutoring and peer support together in one course.

Each course contains proven self-study lessons, each including an introduction, a list of objectives, discussions, practices, self-check tests, and a summary. Users receive online support with the course material from an online tutor. Upon completion, students receive a Certificate of Achievement from edUniverse.

Titles in the edUniverse-University of Nebraska–Lincoln Learning Series include:

Basic Grammar

The Simple Sentence

Modifiers

Understanding Sentences

Choosing the Right Word

Punctuating Sentences Correctly

Intermediate Grammar Series

A Review of Basic Grammar

Clauses

Verbals and Verbal Phrases

A Closer Look at Parts of Speech

Effective Sentences

Basic Mathematics 1
Whole Numbers and their Addition
Subtraction of Whole Numbers
Multiplication of Whole Numbers
Division of Whole Numbers
Exponents, Estimating, Rounding, and Order
Prime Numbers and Factors

Basic Mathematics 2
The Whole Numbers
Addition of Fractions and Mixed Numbers
Subtraction of Fractions
Multiplying and Dividing with Fractions
The Meaning, Addition, and Subtraction of Decimals
Multiplication and Division of Decimals, Problems with Money and Percent

Epilogue

The Future of On-Demand Publishing

E-commerce is exploding and books are the number one online purchase.

Traditional book publishers are narrowing their focus and the number of titles they produce yearly is dropping.

On-demand printing was up 50% in 1997 to $10.5 billion and is forecasted to reach $32 billion by 2002.

toExcel will publish over 50,000 titles in 2002.

What does the future hold? For individual authors and anyone else tired of submitting a manuscript over the transom, predicting the future is never easy. Predicting the future in an industry like publishing, where new technology is changing all the ground rules, is all the more difficult. But that doesn't mean we can't make a few educated guesses as to what the publishing world will look like five years from now.

The easiest prediction to make is that the Internet will grow in importance. Online booksellers has changed the way books are sold over the last few years, and by doing so have turned a lot of publishers on to the power of the Web. No longer just a toy for computer geeks, the Web has finally become a place to do business—a worldwide retail outlet that people are finally willing to use. Will it mean the death of traditional bookstores? Probably not. But it could mean that books won't have to fight for limited space in bookstore windows to become bestsellers. It's only a matter of time before a best-selling author credits the Web for the majority of her sales.

Some people are willing to push this prediction even further and suggest that the days of the traditional paper and ink book are numbered. Instead, they suggest, authors and publishers will store their books on the Web. Buyers will pay to download the book to a personal reader—a small lightweight device capable of storing and displaying books on a computer-like screen. Far-fetched? Maybe. But several companies have already put together prototypes of personal readers. They have many obstacles to overcome—it's still easier to read a real book—but they are willing to spend a lot of money to make this technology viable. So don't count them out too quickly. If the technology can work, the cost of producing a book will plummet.

Of course, the success of any new technology is dependent upon society's acceptance of it. And people still seem very happy with the traditional book technology of paper and ink. They can read them on the beach, on an airplane, in bed, or in the bathtub—so why change the way books are printed?

But technology will change the publishing industry. In a global economy, where companies are constantly looking for new ways to pare down expenses, the wasteful ways of traditional publishing economics must change. Too much money is spent on transporting and warehousing books, and too many books are returned to their publishers to be pulped and turned into new books. The level of waste is enormous. While companies were able to live with wasteful economics in the past—everyone else was dealing with the same situation—they will have to change their ways in the future as new technologies change the playing field.

toExcel is leading the way in using new technology to create new economic scenarios, which in turn create new opportunities. We have created a platform that allows authors who are unable to find a traditional publisher to get their books professionally published for sale around the world.

Our platform can also be used to bring out-of-print books back to life and make sure that books that are published today need never enter the publishing purgatory of out-of-print, out-of-stock.

These new opportunities for authors and publishers will mean a windfall for readers and researchers. They will have easy access to books that would have proven very difficult to track down in the past. Everything from old out-of-print textbooks to new foreign-language novels will be available to anyone with online access, or through any major bookstore in the United States through special order.

These new opportunities represent perhaps the biggest change the publishing industry has seen since Gutenberg invented the printing press. There is now no reason for aspiring authors not to get their books into print. And book sales are no longer dictated by international borders or artificial time lines that see many new publications taken off the shelves just a few months after they are printed.

Publishers can now spend the time, energy, and money acquiring the best quality books available while toExcel takes care of the dirty work of printing, distribution, and sales.

"The dream" that was once just a fantasy for most aspiring authors is now achievable. Keeping books in print forever is an option. In fact, there is no longer any reason for a writer not to get his work published and have it available for anyone who wants to buy it. The economics and limited opportunities that once prevented success have been eliminated. "The dream" has been realized.

Appendix

toExcel Publishing Services Procedures (rev. 3/22/99)

Note: The following procedures and guidelines are for reference only. Please refer to the toExcel Web site for the latest versions of all information, publishing information and title submission forms.

Publishing Services Procedures

1.0 Introduction
2.0 Title Specifications
    2.1 Production Specifications
        2.1.1 Trim Sizes
        2.1.2 Paper Quality
        2.1.3 Book Design
        2.1.4 Cover Design
        2.1.5 New Book Submission
            2.1.5.1 Digital Manuscript Submission Requirements
            2.1.5.2 Manuscript Preparation Guidelines
                2.1.5.2.1 The Parts of a Book
                2.1.5.2.2 Some Basic Text Formatting Rules
        2.1.6 Existing Book Submission
            2.1.6.1 Existing Book Submission Requirements
    2.2 Pricing
3.0 Submitting a Title to toExcel
    3.1 Authors with Manuscripts
        3.1.1 Submission Package
            3.1.1.1 Publishing Agreement (People's Press)
            3.1.1.2 Title Submission Form (Manuscript)
            3.1.1.3 Manuscript
            3.1.1.4 Payment for Publishing Services
        3.1.2 Benefits
    3.2 Authors with Out-of-Print Books
        3.2.1 Submission Package
            3.2.1.1 Publishing Agreement (Out-of-Print)
            3.2.1.2 Title Submission Form (Author)
            3.2.1.3 Books
        3.2.2 Benefits
    3.3 Publishers
        3.3.1 International Publishers
            3.3.1.1 Submission Package
                3.3.1.1.1 Publishing Agreement (International Titles)
                3.3.1.1.2 Title Submission Form (Publisher)
                3.3.1.1.3 Books
            3.3.1.2 Benefits

3.3.2 University Presses
    3.3.2.1 Submission Package
        3.3.2.1.1 Publishing Agreement (University Press)
        3.3.2.1.2 Title Submission Form (Publisher)
        3.3.2.1.3 Books
    3.3.2.2 Benefits
3.3.3 Traditional Publishers (Independent and Mass-Market)
    3.3.3.1 Submission Package
        3.3.3.1.1 Publishing Agreement (per case)
        3.3.3.1.2 Title Submission Form (Publisher)
        3.3.3.1.3 Books
    3.3.3.2 Benefits

1.0 Introduction

toExcel provides on-demand publishing services to authors and publishers in cooperation with its strategic partner, Lightning Print, Inc., a division of Ingram Books. toExcel creates a complete set of digital files for existing and new books from authors and publishers. These files are stored electronically and may be printed, one-at-a-time, as booksellers, authors, publishers or institutions order them. On-demand publishing allows publishers to limit the cost of inventory, order processing, and handling of lower volume titles. Publishers and authors are therefore able to keep more titles in print for the consumer and generate more profits from each title. Authors can have their manuscripts published quickly and easily.

Publishers and authors provide books to toExcel in original hard copy (existing books) or digital files (**new books**).

Existing books are scanned, a proof copy is printed, quality is assured by toExcel, and the title file is stored in the toExcel digital library.

New books are professionally designed in Quark XPress 4.0 to meet toExcel specifications for printing, a proof copy is printed and quality assured by toExcel, and the title is stored in the toExcel digital library.

Orders for books in the toExcel digital library are taken by telephone, fax, our Web site, and from online and brick and mortar bookstores ordering via the Ingram Books database and are printed and shipped directly to the customer when ordered. Semi-annually, toExcel pays the author or publisher an agreed upon royalty upon net receipts for each unit sold.

On-Demand Publishing Work Flow

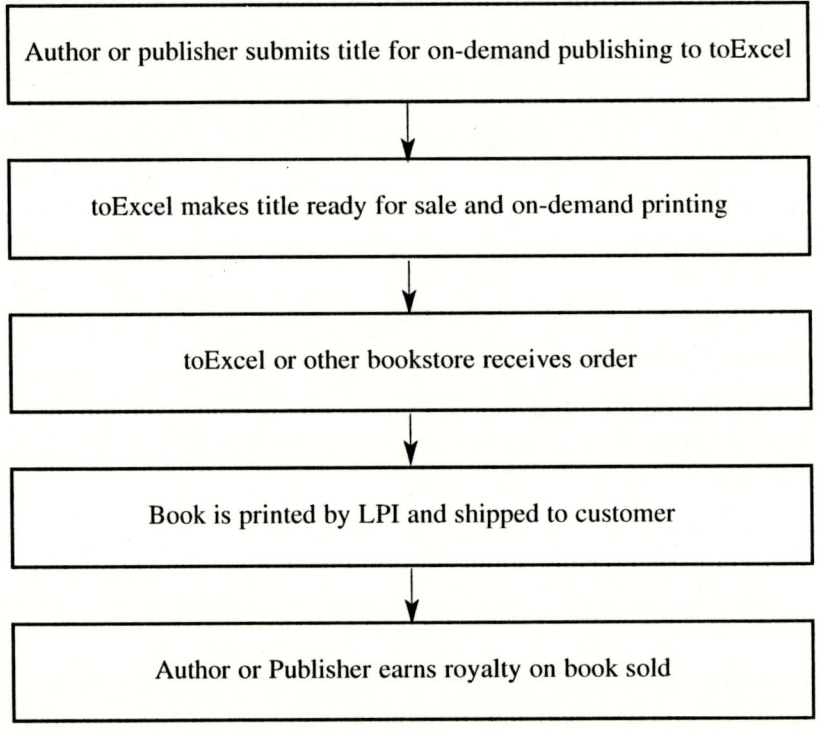

2.0 Title Specifications

There are two general categories of toExcel books based on the characteristics of the book: new and existing.

Each category has unique characteristics that imply marketing designations, unique publishing agreements and title submission forms.

New Books

New books published by toExcel are those created from new, **digital** manuscripts the rights to which are owned by the author. This category is known as the People's Press.

Existing Books

Existing books republished by toExcel are those created by scanning out-of-print, hard copy books. This category is divided according to the rights-holder and for marketing purposes into

Out-of Print/Author: books created by scanning out-of-print, hard copy books the rights to which have reverted to the author.

Out-of Print/Publisher: books created by scanning out-of-print books the rights to which are held by the publisher. This category is divided into:

- **International Publishers**: books unavailable in North America in languages other than English, the rights to which are owned by the publisher. (May include titles that are in-print in the country of origin.)

- **University Press**: out-of-print books from a university press, the rights to which are owned by the publisher.

- **Traditional Publishers**: out-of-print books, the rights to which are owned by the independent, mass-market publisher.

2.1 Production Specifications

2.1.1 Trim Sizes

toExcel produces books in four standard trim sizes

- 5" x 8"
- 5½" x 8½"
- 6" x 9"
- 7½" x 9¼"

2.1.2 Paper Quality

The 5"x 8", 5½" x 8½" and 6" x 9" books will be printed on 60lb offset, opaque, 480 PPI, crème white acid-free paper. The 7½" x 9¼" books will be printed on 50lb offset, opaque, 500 PPI, white acid-free paper. Covers will be printed on white, 80-lb offset, enamel paper and laminated.

2.1.3 Book Design

New toExcel books are designed from digital manuscripts provided by authors using QuarkXPress 4.0. Republished toExcel books are copies of the original book with the addition of a new copyright page and other minor changes as desired by the author or publisher.

All to Excel books carry the name toExcel and the primary cities in which it does business on the title page.

2.1.4 Cover Design

Cover for new books (or books for which the rights to the cover design are not held by the signatory of the Publishing Agreement) are designed using QuarkXPress 4.0, PhotoShop 5.0 and both stock and original graphics. Each cover is unique and based on the suggestions provided by the author in the title submission form.

Covers for existing books (for which the rights to the cover design are held by the signatory of the Publishing Agreement) are copies of the original book cover with the deletion of old barcodes and other minor changes

All toExcel books currently carry the logo of toExcel and LPI on the back cover along with the new barcode.

2.1.5 New Book Submission

Titles accepted for publication by toExcel must meet minimum submission requirements for suitability of content and format. toExcel will not publish hate speech or pornography and reserves the right to reject any manuscript.

2.1.5.1 Digital Manuscript Submission Requirements

Read our Digital Manuscript Submission Guidelines carefully. E-mail any questions to **submissions@toexcel.com**.

- Download (or call/write for) and sign two copies of the Publishing Agreement (People's Press).

- Download (or call/write for) and complete the Title Submission Form (Manuscript.)

- Send two signed copies of your Publishing Agreement (People's Press)., the completed Title Submission Form (Manuscript), a copy of your manuscript, and your check payable to Kaleidoscope Software/toExcel for $299 to

Submissions
Kaleidoscope Software/toExcel
2875 Moorpark Ave., Ste. 208
San Jose, CA 95128

Your manuscript must be:

Fully-edited

Every writer needs an editor. Have your work carefully edited (by friends, family or a professional) before you send it to toExcel. Be sure it is in final, publishable form.

Proof-read

The final copy we receive of your edited manuscript should be proofread by several people who've never seen it before. They have "fresh eyes" and will catch mistakes that you never can.

A non-returnable copy

Do not send us your only copy of your final manuscript. We will not return it.

In one file

Your manuscript should be in one file laid out in 8.5" x11" size in portrait orientation. Please do not separate chapters or sections into several files. Separate chapters by inserting a page break. We need to see how your manuscript should flow from the half-title page to the Index! (you do not need to include Front matter in your file unless you have specific text for it, Acknowledgements, Preface or Dedication, for example

For PC

Sorry, we accept only PC files.

In MS Word or WordPerfect

Versions 5.1 and above

Delivered via media we can read

toExcel accepts files via e-mail attachment, 3.5" floppy disc (PC only), zip disc (PC only), or CD.

With book graphics embedded or noted with placeholders

All graphics in the interior of the book must be of good quality, high-resolution, and in black and white. tif files are preferred. You may embed the graphics in the file to show where you want them placed, or you may type a placeholder. Example: (Graphic file cat.tif here) There must be a corresponding file named **cat.tif** submitted with your manuscript. Graphics files may be submitted via the same media as above.

**With cover graphics included or suggested
in the title submission form**

If you have color or black and white graphics files (for which you own the rights or have permission to use) please include them with your submission. Be sure to include a description of the cover you have in mind in the title submission form. toExcel's designers will use your files and suggestions to create a cover that will sell your book.

108 to 740 Pages after production

Because toExcel books are perfect bound, they must be no shorter than 108 pages and no longer than 740 pages after being designed by toExcel. If your manuscript is fewer than 20,000 words, we may have to add blank pages to reach the 108-page minimum. If the manuscript is over 300,000 words, we may have to produce it in two volumes. Since you will submit your manuscript as an 8.5" x 11" document, you cannot be certain of its final length until after we design it. We will let you know if there is a problem.

2.1.5.2 Manuscript Preparation Guidelines

In order to make your book look as accurate and complete as possible, it's up to you to make the digital text as good as it can be. It is assumed that you have completely edited, spell-checked, and proofread your manuscript several times. The following guidelines should help you further enhance your book.

2.1.5.2.1 The Parts of a Book

Half-title Page

The half-title page of a toExcel book will include the complete book title and the author's name. The back of this page is blank.

Title Page

The title page of a toExcel book must include the complete book title, the author's name and toExcel's publisher information. The back of the title page is the copyright page.

Copyright Page

The copyright page must include the following elements:

Title

All Rights Reserved. Copyright © Date Copyright Holder

No part of this book may be reproduced or transmitted in any form or by any means, graphic, electronic, or mechanical, including photocopying, recording, taping, or by any information storage or retrieval system, without the permission in writing from the publisher.

Published by toExcel
For information address:

toExcel

165 West 95th Street, Suite B-N
New York, NY 10025
www.toExcel.com

ISBN: 1-58348-115-X
Printed in the United States of America
0 9 8 7 6 5 4 3 2 1

Front and Back Matter

You may include any front and/or back matter including acknowledgements, dedication, preface, introduction, or table of illustrations. Be sure to include all front and back matter in the actual manuscript file and in the order in which you wish it to appear.

Please do not include page numbers in your table of contents, illustrations or index. All we need are the items. After we design the text, we will assign the correct page numbers in the table of contents and index the entries you have given us.

Main Body Text

toExcel book designers will create running heads for and number each page of your book.

Cover

toExcel covers are printed on a four-color digital press. Please offer any suggestions as to colors, images or designs you would like. Our designers will incorporate your ideas. If you have a graphic in .tif format to which you own the rights and would like us to use, please enclose it and our designers will work with it. If you do not have a digital file of the art you wish to use, toExcel can create one at an extra charge.

Please supply text for the back cover as well. However, toExcel retains the right to edit back cover text as necessary.

Please supply all the information on the title submission form.

2.1.5.2.2 Some Basic Text Formatting Rules

toExcel book designers follow the rules of *The Chicago Manual of Style*. Our own design guide is based on Robin Williams' book, *The Non-Designers Design Book*. Both of these books are available from any major bookstore and are invaluable references.

Consistency in Using the Title

If you will be referring often to a book or other title, be consistent in your formatting. For example, if the title of your book is *Man Before Adam: A Correction to Doctrinal Theology*, always spell and format it the same way. Shortening the title once it's been established is fine. Once we know the title is *Man Before Adam: A Correction to Doctrinal Theology*, we know what you mean when you write it as is *Man Before Adam*, but do not write it later in the book *as Man Before Adam: A Correction To Doctrinal Theology*. Be absolutely consistent in your spelling and capitalization.

Section Breaks

Generally speaking, toExcel designers do not need to see section breaks in the manuscript. A simple inserted page break will let us know where the end of the section occurs

Page Breaks

Please do not insert page breaks at the end of what you feel is a "page" in the body text. Since your manuscript is delivered to us in a word-processing application (MS Word® or WordPerfect®) as an 8.5" x 11" document, the length of the pages will not be the same when the book is designed in a 6" x 9" Quark file. You may insert page breaks at the end of chapters or sections if you feel that the end of a section may not be clear.

Graphics

Please embed graphics within your MS Word® or WordPerfect® file or type a placeholder that matches exactly the title of the graphics file you have enclosed with your manuscript submission. **Graphics should be in tif format.** Graphics in .bmp format cannot easily be sized. .jpeg files may be included for cover art, but note that low resolution graphics (gifs and jpegs) may not print well.

Punctuation

One space after all punctuation. View the number of spaces, hard carriage returns and other "invisibles" by clicking the paragraph symbol (¶) on the MS Word® toolbar or the Reveal Codes selection in WordPerfect®.

Do not use double dashes (—) or hyphens (-) to express a pause in a thought or duration of time.

Use **em dashes** (—) or **ellipses** (…) to separate thoughts or clauses within a sentence.

Use **en dashes** (–) to separate periods of time or numbers.

> Dashes, ellipses and other special characters are found under the Insert menu under Symbol/Special Characters in MS Word®.

Use **hyphens** (-) to separate words.

Examples of correct usage:

Em Dash
I wanted to go—in fact I needed to go—but I just couldn't get away.

He went to the store—and he's not coming back.

Ellipsis
I wanted to go…in fact I needed to go…but I just couldn't get away.

He went to the store…and he's not coming back

Ellipses are also used to indicate missing text.

When Jesus asked Peter, "Who and I?" and Jesus answered, "…flesh and blood hath not revealed it unto thee, but my Father which is in heaven. …upon this rock will I build my church." (example from *The Chicago Manual of Style*)

En Dash
The war lasted from 1889–1902.

We will be at the party from 2:00 P.M.–3:00 P.M.

(Note, too, the traditional use of "small caps" for the designations a.m. and p.m. Choose small caps under the MS Word® Format/Font menu)

Hyphen
She was twenty-five years old.

That idea was really half-baked.

Other Formatting Suggestions
- Always use curly or "smart quotes" as opposed to straight quotes (straight quotes look like inch marks (" "). You can find smart quotes and other useful characters and symbols under the Special Characters list in MS Word® or use them automatically by selecting AutoCorrect/AutoFormat/Replace Straight Quotes with Smart Quotes" in the Tools menu. In WordPerfect®, type smart quotes automatically by choosing Tools/Quick Correct/Options. Turn on smart singe and double quotes.
- Limit use of all caps. WORDS TYPED IN ALL CAPS ARE DIFFICULT TO READ.
- Limit use of underlining. Underlined text usually looks *old-fashioned*. To emphasize text, use bold.
- Limit use of centered text. It looks formal and can be hard to read.
- Format book, magazine article, and other titles per *The Chicago Manual of Style*.

- Format bibliography entries per *The Chicago Manual of Style*.
- Punctuate carefully. Punctuation almost always falls within quotation marks. Example:
- When Jesus asked Peter, "Who am I?" and Jesus answered, "…flesh and blood hath not revealed it unto thee, but my Father which is in heaven. …upon this rock will I build my church." (example from *The Chicago Manual of Style*)
- You may use two returns to indicate space between paragraphs, but note that toExcel replaces double "carriage returns" (paragraph markings ¶) with appropriate space after paragraph.
- Please indent paragraphs with tab characters not spaces.

2.1.6 Existing Book Submission

Titles accepted for publication by toExcel must meet minimum submission requirements for suitability of content and format. toExcel will not publish hate speech or pornography and reserves the right to reject any manuscript.

2.1.6.1 Existing Book Submission Requirements

Read our Book Submission Guidelines carefully. E-mail any questions to **submissions@toexcel.com**

- Download (or call/write for) and sign two copies of the Publishing Agreement (Author, International Titles or University Press.)
- Download (or call/write for) and complete the Title Submission Form (Author or Publisher) for each title.
- Send two signed copies of your Publishing Agreement, the completed Title Submission Forms(s), and two copies of each book to:

Submissions
Kaleidoscope Software/toExcel
2875 Moorpark Ave., Ste. 208
San Jose, CA 95128

Books Must Meet Size Requirements

toExcel will decide in which trim size your existing book will be republished based on the following table.

For Trim Size	Original Text Paper Size Must Be	Original Text Print Size Must Be
5" x 8"	Width 4.125" to 6.125"	Max Width 4.375"
	Length 7.25' to 9.25"	Max Length 7.5"
5½" x 8½"	Width 4.625" to 6.625"	Max Width 4.875"
	Length 7.75" to 9.75"	Max Length 8"
6" x 9"	Width 5.125" to 7.125"	Max Width 5.375"
	Length 8.25" to 10.25"	Max Length 8.5"
7½" x 9¼"	Width 6.625" to 8.625"	Max Width 6.875"

Number of copies

toExcel needs **two copies** of each title you want to republish.

Books must be in good condition

The quality of our reproduction of your book is determined by the quality of existing book hard copy you give us. We can improve some aspects of the book, such as removing stray dots or marks and restoring the color of the cover. However, we cannot improve the quality of the original printing, either of text or halftones.

Books are non-returnable

We will not be able to return either copy of your original book. One is destroyed in making the digital files of the book. One is necessary for our reference.

Books must be 108 to 740 pages after production

Because toExcel books are perfect bound, they must be no shorter than 108 pages and no longer than 740 pages after being designed by toExcel. If your book is fewer than 108 total pages, we may have to add blank pages to reach the 108-page minimum. If the book is over 740 pages, we will have to produce it in two volumes and sell each volume separately. For an example, see Danny Goodman's Complete HyperCard Handbook on the toExcel site.

Submit Cover Graphics and Back Cover Text

If you own the rights to the original art and design of the cover of your out-of-print book, toExcel can update that cover for your new book. If you do not, we will create a new cover for your book. If you have color graphic files (for which you own the rights or have permission to use them) please include these files with your title submission form, along with a description of the cover you have in mind. toExcel's designers will use your files and suggestions to create a cover that complements your book. Please be sure to include suggested back cover text for your new cover.

Books Should Contain No Color Graphics and Limited Halftone Graphics

toExcel cannot currently print color graphics or text in its books. If more than 10% of the pages of your book contain halftones, extra time will be needed to republish your book.

Making Changes

toExcel makes limited changes to republished books. Commonly, we remove old barcodes and ISBNs as well as statements of paper durability or printing credits that do not apply to your newly republished title. We also create a new copyright page that gives the correct ISBN and publishing information. For an example, please see the Columbia University book Critical Genealogies on the toExcel site.

Copyright Page

Since we are republishing your book, we will assign a new ISBN and create a new copyright page. For an example, please see the Columbia University Press book Critical Genealogies on the toExcel site.

The new copyright page will generally include the following elements:

Title

All Rights Reserved. Copyright © Date Copyright Holder

No part of this book may be reproduced or transmitted in any form or by any means, graphic, electronic, or mechanical, including photocopying, recording, taping, or by any information storage or retrieval system, without the permission in writing from the publisher.

Published by toExcel.*
For information address:

toExcel

165 West 95th Street, Suite B-N
New York, NY 10025
www.toExcel.com

ISBN: 1-58348-115-X

Printed in the United States of America

0 9 8 7 6 5 4 3 2 1

*If rights are owned by the publisher, this line will read, "Published by toExcel in cooperation with (publisher name)."

2.2 Pricing

toExcel sets all prices for books it published based on the following criteria:

Existing Books: Prices for books republished from existing books are based on the price of the original book. If the book has been out-of-print long enough to make the original price invalid, pricing is determined based upon competitive market prices for the category.

New Books: Prices for books published from new manuscripts are based upon competitive market prices for the category.

3.0 Submitting a Title to toExcel

Authors and Publishers may submit titles to toExcel by sending their complete submission packages via mail or e-mail attachment following the instructions below and the submission guidelines outlined in sections 2.1.5 and 2.1.6 above or on the toExcel site at www.toExcel.com.

3.1 Authors with Manuscripts

3.1.1 Submission Package

Author with manuscripts should submit a complete submission package. The package includes:

- Two signed copies of the completed Publishing Agreement (People's Press).
- The completed Title Submission Form (Manuscript).
- A properly formatted copy of the manuscript.
- Payment in the amount of $299 payable to Kaleidoscope Software/toExcel, Inc.

The complete submission package should be sent to:

Submissions
Kaleidoscope Software/toExcel
2875 Moorpark Ave., Ste. 208
San Jose, CA 95128

E-mail any questions or information about e-mail submission to **submissions@toexcel.com**.

3.1.1.1 Publishing Agreement (People's Press)

Authors with manuscripts should carefully read the Publishing Agreement (People's Press)) available at the toExcel Web site. E-mail any questions to **submissions@toexcel.com**. Carefully complete two copies of the agreement, sign both copies, and return them to toExcel Submissions with your submission package.

A cosigned copy of the agreement will be returned to you by mail when your manuscript has been accepted.

3.1.1.2 Title Submission Form (Manuscript)

Authors with manuscripts should carefully read the Title Submission Form (Manuscript). This document collects all the information toExcel needs to process your book and must be completed satisfactorily before your book goes into production. E-mail any questions to **submissions@toexcel.com**.

Carefully complete the Title Submission Form (Manuscript) and return it to toExcel Submissions with your submission package.

You will be contacted if we need more information.

3.1.1.3 Manuscript

Authors with manuscripts should carefully read section 2.1.5 of this document, New Book Submission, and submit your manuscript file with your submission package.

Manuscripts must conform to the New Book Submission parameters. You will be contacted if there is a problem with your digital file.

Note: Manuscripts will not be reviewed until a complete submission package has been received and approved.

3.1.1.4 Payment for Publishing Services

Authors with manuscripts should enclose payment in the amount of $299 payable to Kaleidoscope Software/toExcel, Inc. with the submission package.

Visa, Master Card, American Express, certified checks and money orders are accepted.

3.1.2 Benefits

Authors whose manuscripts are published by toExcel receive e-commerce, Web marketing and distribution capabilities via the toExcel site; excellent design and production of the book; and inclusion in the Ingram Books database of titles.

For specific information on:
- Author sample books
- royalties and payment
- discount pricing on book orders
- ability to enter into a publishing agreement with another publisher
- Other terms and benefits of the agreement

See agreement available at the toExcel Web site.

3.2 Authors with Out-of-Print Books

3.2.1 Submission Package

Authors with out-of-print books should submit a **complete submission package**. The package includes:

Two signed copies of the completed Publishing Agreement (Out-of-Print).

- The completed Title Submission Form (Author)
- Two copies of the book
- The complete submission package should be sent to:

  Submissions
  Kaleidoscope Software/toExcel
  2875 Moorpark Ave., Ste. 208
  San Jose, CA 95128

E-mail any questions or information about e-mail submission to **submissions@toexcel.com**.

3.2.1.1 Publishing Agreement (Out-of-Print)

Authors with out-of-print books should carefully read the Publishing Agreement (Out-of-Print)) available at the toExcel Web site. E-mail any questions to **submissions@toexcel.com**. Carefully complete two copies of the agreement, sign both copies, and return them to toExcel Submissions with your submission package.

A cosigned copy of the agreement will be returned to you by mail when your book has been accepted.

3.2.1.2 Title Submission Form (Author)

Authors with out-of-print books should carefully read the Title Submission Form (Author) available at the toExcel Web site. This document collects all the information toExcel needs to process your book and must be completed satisfactorily before your book goes into production. E-mail any questions to **submissions@toexcel.com**.

Carefully complete the Title Submission Form (Author) and return it to toExcel Submissions with your submission package.

You will be contacted if we need more information.

3.2.1.3 Books

Authors with out-of-print books should carefully read section 2.1.6 of this document, Existing Book Submission, and submit two copies of your book with your submission package.

Books must conform to the Existing Book Submission parameters. You will be contacted if there is a problem with your book.

* Note: Books will not be put into production until a complete submission package has been received and approved.

3.2.2 Benefits

Authors whose books are republished by toExcel receive e-commerce, Web marketing and distribution capabilities via the toExcel site; excellent reproduction of the book; and inclusion in the Ingram Books database of titles.

For specific information on:

- royalties and payment
- discount pricing on book orders
- ability to enter into a publishing agreement with another publisher
- other terms and benefits of the agreement

See agreement available at the toExcel Web site.

3.3 Publishers

3.3.1 International Publishers

3.3.1.1 Submission Package

International publishers must submit a **complete submission package**. The package includes:

- Two signed copies of the completed Publishing Agreement (International Titles).
- The completed Title Submission Form (Publisher).
- Two copies of the book.

The complete submission package should be sent to:

Submissions
Kaleidoscope Software/toExcel
2875 Moorpark Ave., Ste. 208
San Jose, CA 95128

E-mail any questions or information about e-mail submission to **submissions@toexcel.com**.

3.3.1.1.1 Publishing Agreement (International Titles)

International publishers should carefully read the Publishing Agreement (International)) available at the toExcel Web site. E-mail any questions to **submissions@toexcel.com**. Carefully complete two copies of the agreement, sign both copies, and return them to toExcel Submissions with your submission package.

A cosigned copy of the agreement will be returned to you by mail when your book has been accepted.

3.3.1.1.2 Title Submission Form (Publisher)

International publishers should carefully read the Title Submission Form (Publisher)) available at the toExcel Web site. This document collects all the information toExcel needs to process your book and must be completed satisfactorily before your book goes into production. E-mail any questions to **submissions@toexcel.com**.

Carefully complete the Title Submission Form (Publisher) and return it to toExcel Submissions with your submission package.

You will be contacted if we need more information.

3.3.1.1.3 Books

International publishers should carefully read section 2.1.6 of this document, Existing Book Submission, and submit two copies of your book with your submission package.

Books must conform to the Existing Book Submission parameters. You will be contacted if there is a problem with your book.

* Note: Books will not be put into production until a complete submission package has been received and approved.

3.3.1.2 Benefits

International publishers whose books are republished by toExcel receive e-commerce, Web marketing and distribution capabilities via the toExcel site; excellent reproduction of the book; and inclusion in the Ingram Books database of titles.

For specific information on:

- royalties and payment
- discount pricing on book orders
- Other terms and benefits of the agreement

See agreement available at the toExcel Web site.

3.3.2 University Presses

3.3.2.1 Submission Package

University Presses must submit a **complete submission package**. The package includes:

- Two signed copies of the completed Publishing Agreement (University Presses).

- The completed Title Submission Form (Publisher).
- Two copies of the book.

The complete submission package should be sent to:

**Submissions
Kaleidoscope Software/toExcel
2875 Moorpark Ave., Ste. 208
San Jose, CA 95128**

E-mail any questions or information about e-mail submission to **submissions@toexcel.com**.

3.3.2.1.1 Publishing Agreement (University Presses)

University Presses should carefully read the Publishing Agreement (University Presses)) available at the toExcel Web site. E-mail any questions to **submissions@toexcel.com**. Carefully complete two copies of the agreement, sign both copies, and return them to toExcel Submissions with your submission package.

A cosigned copy of the agreement will be returned to you by mail when your book has been accepted.

3.3.2.1.2 Title Submission Form (Publisher)

University Presses should carefully read the Title Submission Form (Publisher) available at the toExcel Web site. This document collects all the information toExcel needs to process your book and must be completed satisfactorily before your book goes into production. E-mail any questions to **submissions@toexcel.com**.

Carefully complete the Title Submission Form (Publisher) and return it to toExcel Submissions with your submission package.

You will be contacted if we need more information.

3.3.2.1.3 Books

University Presses should carefully read section 2.1.6 of this document, Existing Book Submission, and submit two copies if your book with your submission package.

Books must conform to the Existing Book Submission parameters. You will be contacted if there is a problem with your book.

* **Note: Books will not be put into production until a complete submission package has been received and approved.**

3.3.2.2 Benefits

University Presses whose books are republished by toExcel receive e-commerce, Web marketing and distribution capabilities via the toExcel site; excellent reproduction of the book; and inclusion in the Ingram Books database of titles.

For specific information on:

- royalties and payment
- discount pricing on book orders
- Other terms and benefits of the agreement

See agreement available at the toExcel Web site.

3.3.2 Traditional Publishers

3.3.2.1 Submission Package

Traditional Publishers must submit a **complete submission package**. The package includes:

- Two signed copies of the completed Publishing Agreement (per case).
- The completed Title Submission Form (Publisher).
- Two copies of the book.

The complete submission package should be sent to:

**Submissions
Kaleidoscope Software/toExcel
2875 Moorpark Ave., Ste. 208
San Jose, CA 95128**

E-mail any questions or information about e-mail submission to **submissions@toexcel.com**.

3.3.3.1.1 Publishing Agreement

Traditional publishers may e-mail of phone for information.

3.3.3.1.2 Title Submission Form (Publisher)

Traditional publishers should carefully read the Title Submission Form (Publisher)) available at the toExcel Web site. This document collects all the information toExcel needs to process your book and must be completed satisfactorily before your book goes into production. E-mail any questions to **submissions@toexcel.com**.

Carefully complete the Title Submission Form (Publisher) and return it to toExcel Submissions with your submission package.

You will be contacted if we need more information.

3.3.3.1.3 Books

Traditional publishers should carefully read section 2.1.6 of this document, Existing Book Submission, and submit two copies of your book with your submission package.

Books must conform to the Existing Book Submission parameters. You will be contacted if there is a problem with your book.

* Note: Books will not be put into production until a complete submission package has been received and approved.

3.3.3.2 Benefits

Traditional publishers whose books are republished by toExcel receive e-commerce, Web marketing and distribution capabilities via the toExcel site; excellent reproduction of the book; and inclusion in the Ingram Books database of titles.

For specific information on:

- royalties and payment
- discount pricing on book orders
- Other terms and benefits of the agreement

Call or e-mail toExcel for more information.

VỤ ÁN TRẦN NGỌC CHÂU